THE RENEWAL OF THE CHURCH

THE RENEWAL
OF
THE CHURCH

by

W. A. VISSER 'T HOOFT

THE WESTMINSTER PRESS
PHILADELPHIA

First published in Great Britain in 1956
by the S. C. M. Press, London

Library of Congress Catalogue Card Number: 57-5059

TYPESET IN GREAT BRITAIN
PRINTED IN THE UNITED STATES OF AMERICA

THE DALE LECTURES

THE Dale Lectures were founded to commemorate the services which Robert William Dale (1829-95) rendered to Mansfield College, Oxford. Dr Dale was Minister of Carr's Lane Meeting House, and a very notable figure of both Birmingham and national life in the year 1871 when the University of Oxford was opened to Nonconformists. It was in no small measure due to Dr Dale's advocacy that a decision was taken to open Mansfield College in Oxford in 1886, and to close Spring Hill College, Birmingham, in order to provide some endowment for the new College. Dr Dale was the first to preach a sermon in the College Chapel, during the opening proceedings; and he was elected the first Chairman of the College Council. The lecturers already appointed on the foundation are:

1904   W. M. RAMSEY: The Cities of St Paul.
1907   T. R. GLOVER: The Conflict of Religions in the Roman Empire.
1913   EDWARD C. MOORE, Harvard University: West and East.
1920   J. A. HADFIELD: Psychology and Morals.
1922   ALBERT SCHWEITZER: The Philosophy of Civilization.
1929   ROBERT FRICK, Marburg University.
1933   R. S. FRANKS: The Atonement.
1940   W. F. HOWARD: Christianity according to St John.
1943   H. G. WOOD: Frederick Denison Maurice.
1947   HENRI CLAVIER, Strasbourg University: The Theology of Resistance.
1951   H. A. HODGES: Some Themes for Christian Philosophy.
1953   SIGMUND MOWINCKEL, Uppsala University: Enthronement Festival and the Enthronement Psalms in the History of Israel.
1955   W. A. VISSER'T HOOFT, General Secretary, World Council of Churches: The Renewal of the Church.

FOREWORD

In asking Dr Visser 't Hooft to deliver the 1955 series of Dale Lectures the authorities of the College were recognizing the truth to which the late Dr Temple testified when he spoke of the Ecumenical Movement as one of the great new facts of our time. It seems important that such a Movement should receive careful and scholarly examination, and that those best able to judge it should be invited to speak upon it; the College hoped that when Dr Visser 't Hooft delivered his lectures he would have something relevant to say. The lectures which constitute the book are not indeed a direct examination of the Ecumenical Movement as such; they are a biblical, theological and historical reflection upon the conditions in which a truly ecumenical movement can arise and flourish. Dr Visser 't Hooft's observations will gain weight from his long experience with the Ecumenical Movement, but his office in it does not and cannot make them authoritative or binding. Dr Visser 't Hooft has served the Churches well as an able and devoted Secretary of the World's Student Christian Federation for many years, and, since 1939, as the General Secretary of the World Council of Churches. The College believes that he has done them no less a service in offering these reflections on the essential meaning of renewal in the Church.

The College was happy to have Dr Visser 't Hooft as its guest and lecturer; and proud that, during his stay, the University of Oxford conferred upon him the rare distinction of the degree of Doctor of Divinity, *honoris causa*.

JOHN MARSH

MANSFIELD COLLEGE,
OXFORD
14th December 1955

7

CONTENTS

INTRODUCTION

THESE 'Dale Lectures' were given in Mansfield College, Oxford, in October 1955. In preparing them I have used a good deal of the material prepared for a series of lectures which I gave at the Facultada Evangelica in Buenos Aires in 1952 and which have been published in Spanish.

The reason why I have chosen this particular subject is that there is some danger that the expression 'renewal of the Church' may become an empty slogan. In the period since the last war it has become a very general conviction that in some sense the churches stand in need of renewal. The basic theme of the ecumenical discussion has been and is the rediscovery of the Church as the new people of God. Now this conversation between the churches forces each church to ask in which ways it must be renewed in order to be the Church in the real sense of that word. And wherever Christian men and women consider the task of the Church in relation to the modern world, they come to the conclusion that it is only a radically transformed Church that can fulfil that task.

But there has been little reflection on the nature of the renewal that we seek. And it is hard to find any helpful literature which discusses the question at the level at which it deserves to be discussed.

I felt therefore that it was time to raise some basic questions about the meaning of renewal. It is, of course, clear to me that these lectures do no more than open up this great subject and I hope that others, who have more time for serious theological work than a World Council of Churches' secretary, will enter into that discussion and throw light upon many points which I have not treated adequately.

I realize that the expression 'renewal of the Church' can easily be misunderstood and that in two ways.

Renewal can be taken to mean mere innovation, the creation of something different for the sake of change or for the sake of adaptation to the most recent historical developments. I trust that the lectures on the biblical concept of renewal will show that I do not believe that the Christian Church is concerned with novelty *per se* or with synchronizing its message with the spirit of the times, but that its point of reference is the newness of the new age inaugurated by the coming of Christ.

Similarly the renewal of the Church can be taken to mean the replacing of the Church which began at Pentecost, by some newly invented religious institution or movement. But is it really necessary to say that the Church which is the Body of Christ need not and cannot be renewed and that therefore, if we speak of the renewal of the Church this can only mean the renewal of the Church as it lives in history? This historical Church as it exists in the form of the churches, needs renewal because an unrenewed Church obscures and denies the faith that the Body belongs to the living Christ, who is the Head.

When the reform-councils spoke of the need for 'reformation of the Church in its head and members' no one took this to mean that they sought to deny the 'givenness' of the Church or that they sought to create another Church. Similarly to speak of the renewal of the Church does not mean to deny that the Church against which the gates of Hades will not prevail is one and the same Church through the centuries.

But it happens that we have only one single word to cover at the same time the *Una Sancta* which needs no renewal and the Church in history which stands constantly in need of renewal. And to use the word Church only in the sense of *Una Sancta* means to condemn ourselves to silence concerning the empirical life of the Church. I believe that there is biblical authority for this terminology. We must avoid the 'angelic fallacy' which St Augustine repudiated when he said that the Church here on earth is not without spot or wrinkle and needs to pray: 'Forgive us our sins.' I hope therefore that the title of these lectures will rightly be interpreted as the renewal of the Church in its historical existence, as the *ecclesia peccatorum*.

It is not unnecessary to add that I am alone responsible for the views expressed in these lectures. For it happens sometimes that the personal opinions of the General Secretary of the World Council of Churches are taken as in some sense representing the views of the World Council itself. Those who know the World Council from within will make no such mistake. For they realize that a World Council opinion is the outcome of a long process of conversation and interaction between persons of many different ecclesiastical and theological backgrounds and that no one person can ever speak for the World Council unless he has submitted his opinions to that long process.

Finally I should like to use this opportunity to express my gratitude to Mansfield College and especially to its Principal Dr John Marsh for making me feel so much at home that I began to wonder whether the life of a 'don' in Oxford is not preferable to the life of an itinerant ecumenical secretary.

I

THE OLD COVENANT AND
ITS RENEWAL

HAS the record of the dealings of God with the people of Israel any immediate relevance for a study of the renewal of the Church? Some have answered this question by saying that the Old Testament is not only irrelevant for the Church today, but that the influence which it exerts upon the Church is a sign of ecclesiastical paralysis. But that answer is theologically wrong and historically untrue. It is theologically wrong because the Church is the people of God and that basic definition does not mean that the Church has as it were stolen a title which belonged originally to another people, but that the Church of Christ is the rightful successor to Israel and stands with Israel in one and the same continuous history governed by one and the same design of God. When the Church reflects on the renewal of its own life it must therefore begin by remembering how the life of the people of God under the Old Covenant has been renewed again and again.

At the same time it is a historical fact that the significance which the Church ascribes to the history of the people of Israel has a decisive bearing on its conception of the renewal of its own life. In the New Testament itself the memory of God's ways of dealing with his people in the old days is an *idée-force*, the dynamic element in the exhortation to live up to the promises of God. 'These things', says Paul referring to the experiences of the fathers, 'happened to them as a warning (literally, typically), but they were written down for our instruction' (I Cor. 10.11). And in the history of the Church the realization of the actual and immediate meaning of the story of Israel for the Church has again and again been a force of renewal, while the notion that that story merely belonged to the past has been an obstacle to renewal.

What then has the Old Testament to say on this subject? The account which the Old Testament itself gives of the dealings between the people of Israel and their God is characterized by an astounding lack of self-delusion. Which other people has ever recorded its own past with such merciless realism? In his lectures on *Christianity and History*[1] Professor Butterfield remarks that what was unique about the ancient Hebrews was their historiography rather than their history and that not only in that it saw the hand of God in events, but also 'in that it ascribed the successes of Israel not to virtue, but to the favour of God; and instead of narrating the glories or demonstrating the righteousness of the nation, like our modern patriotic histories, it denounced the infidelity of the people, denounced it not as an occasional thing but as the constant feature of the nation's conduct throughout the centuries. . . .' It is not surprising that in a much later period the rabbis who sought to present Jewish history as the record of a people which had lived up to its claims and privileges, have sought to soften the sharp contours and to give it a more innocent character.[2] But the original account remains. It is a history of a people which 'murmurs' against the God who seeks to save it.

Now it is remarkable that this realistic appraisal of the

[1] P. 73.

[2] Rengstorf gives a number of examples of this attempt at reinterpretation in Kittel, I, 731-2.

people and the grateful recognition of God's amazing patience in his dealings with them is to be found in all layers of biblical literature, so that it is in a very real sense a *leitmotiv* of the Old Testament. In the Books of Exodus and Numbers the stories that go back to the old Jahvistic and Elohistic sources tell us that the murmuring begins almost immediately after the liberation of the people from Egypt. As soon as the armies of Pharaoh have disappeared the people become rebellious. And this murmuring becomes the keyword in the description of the desert journey. The Epistle of the Hebrews does not exaggerate when it says that all who left Egypt under the leadership of Moses provoked God (Heb. 3.16). For their 'murmuring' does not simply mean that they were dissatisfied. They were not simply grumbling as travelling parties are in the habit of grumbling against their 'dragoman' or tour leader. Theirs was a fundamental protest against God. Moses says: 'Your murmurings are not against us, but against the Lord' (Ex. 16.8). The people believe that they are entitled to the divine protection and that God does not fulfil his part of the contract.[1]

In the early prophets the same theme appears. Thus Hosea describes the tragedy of the unfaithfulness of Israel in terms of adultery. Israel is the faithless wife who betrays her loving husband to whom she owes everything (2.4-8). But God will judge her and convince her of her sin. And there will be a new, an eternal betrothal (2.19).

When we come to the deuteronomic literature we find that this point of view has developed into a full-fledged theology of history. For the Book of Deuteronomy and the literature dependent on it do not only describe specific cases of the rebellion of the people against God; they present the

[1] The translation 'grumbling' in the R.S.V. (e.g. I Cor. 10.10) obscures the radical nature of the protest.

whole of Jewish history as a continuous series of rebellions and they state explicitly how these rebellions are to be viewed in the light of God's dealings with his people.

This becomes particularly clear in the Book of Judges. For it gives us both a clear-cut statement concerning the theological presuppositions of its author or authors and a typical example of historiography based on such presuppositions. In the second chapter of the Book (verses 11 to 23) we have the deuteronomic view of history in a nut-shell. It is a radically theocentric view according to which the history of Israel proceeds in rhythmic cycles. Each generation passes through the same stages. These stages can be described as follows: (1) The starting point is 'the great works of the Lord that he did for Israel' (2.7); (2) The people forsake the Lord and provoke him to anger; (3) The Lord delivers them into the hands of their enemies; (4) The people are distressed and cry unto the Lord (see 3.9; 3.15, etc.); (5) the Lord delivers the people.

Now this scheme is not merely a general introduction to the history of the Judges. It is systematically applied to the events of the period in such a way that each is somehow fitted into the general framework and that each individual story serves to bring out the same basic truth concerning the faithful God and his unfaithful people. It is obvious that this kerugmatic historiography applied in such a radical and schematic manner does not give the most trustworthy answers to the modern question: What exactly happened at that time? But it remains a *kerugma*, a strong witness to the people of God at all times. For, even though we cannot conceive of the cycle of history in quite the same schematic way as the deuteronomic authors, it remains a spiritual fact that the people of God go again and again through the stages of forsaking their Lord, of subservience to false gods, of deliverance through judgment and of renewal of obedience.

In the later stages of Old Testament literature we find the same view of history. The most moving and striking examples are the ninth chapter of the Book of Nehemiah and the seventy-eighth Psalm. Both authors present in different ways, though sometimes in similar words, exactly the same picture. We are again struck by the complete lack of illusions concerning the attitude of the fathers. There is not the slightest trace of hero-worship or of glorification of the past. For the only criterion which counts for these unusual historians is how the people have responded to the great deeds of God in their life. And as they apply that standard, they find that the history of their nation is characterized by unimaginable ingratitude and disobedience to the God to whom it owes everything.

Both passages begin with strong statements about God's mighty works undertaken for the sake of his chosen people. But neither the Levites in the Book of Nehemiah nor the Psalmist have anything to say about a grateful response of the people. On the contrary! Both have to continue with the tragic and finally monotonous story of the innumerable occasions when Israel refused to obey. Both records are dominated by a rich vocabulary of expressions indicating the fundamentally rebellious attitude of the people to their God. They 'dealt proudly'; they 'hardened their necks'; they 'wrought great provocations'; they 'did evil again' before God; they were 'stubborn'; they 'forgot' God's works; they 'tempted' God and 'trusted not in his salvation'. The indictment is complete and there are no extenuating circumstances. When Stephen in his address before the High Priest (recorded in the seventh chapter of Acts) concludes: 'Ye stiff-necked and uncircumcised in heart and ears, ye do always resist the Holy Ghost; as your fathers did, so do ye'—he is not saying something new and unheard of; he only reminds the Jewish leaders of the truth about their own history which is contained in their own Holy Scripture.

But our passages show equally clearly the other side of the picture. It is that in spite of the interminable series of acts of rebellion God continues to work at the salvation of his people. The monotony of their record of disobedience is interrupted by the interventions of the Lord, who does not allow his people to forget him, who shakes them with his judgment and gives them another chance through his forgiveness. And so in the darkness of the record of rebellion there shines the light of the record of God's deeds. Deeds of judgment: he 'delivers them into the hands of their enemies', his 'wrath comes upon them'. But also and above all deeds of mercy: He does not 'forsake them'; he gives his 'Spirit to instruct them', for he 'remembers that they are but flesh'. And the purpose of the judgment is salvation for, as the Psalm puts it, 'when he slew them, then they sought him and then they returned (to him) and inquired early after God'. In other words God's wrath expressed in the punishments which he brings upon the people is in reality an expression of the patient love by which he seeks to restore the broken relationship.

Now all this finds its simplest and clearest expression in that it is said of God that he makes and keeps the Covenant and that it is said of the people that they are not steadfast in the Covenant and do not keep it. Thus the whole story of Israel can be described as the dramatic dialogue between the Maker of the Covenant and the breakers of the Covenant.

The Covenant which God had made with Israel was never meant as a provisional agreement which could be denounced whenever one of them happened to be tired of it. In fact it was not an agreement such as men make with each other.

For the parties which concluded it were not on the same plane. From the side of God the Covenant is an act of pure grace by which he chooses Israel as 'his people of inheritance', that is as his own people. The very expression shows that we have to do with a divine initiative and that God remains the undisputed master of the situation. From the side of man the Covenant is the acknowledgment of God's promise and God's gift and the acceptance of his unconditional sovereignty as Ruler of the nation. We must therefore not allow ourselves to be misled by the word 'covenant' to think of a bilateral contract between two equal parties. For that was precisely the sin of Israel. Again and again they came to believe that on the basis of the Covenant they were entitled to claim their rights before God and to expect to be treated as the most favoured nation and then according to their own notion of what was good for them. In fact the Covenant is an ordinance of God which implies only one right and one privilege: that is to serve God and to live in communion with him, but which creates at the same time the dangerous situation of being the special object of his holy concern. Amos shows these two sides of the Covenant when he prophesies: 'You only have I known of all the families of the earth; *therefore* will I punish you for all your iniquities' (Amos 3.2).

What has all this to do with the renewal of the Church? We have learned that the story of God's people is the story of a stubborn and stiff-necked people who forget again and again who they are and what is the true meaning of their existence. They are set apart to be a holy people and have no other *raison d'être* than the service of God. They accept that mission, but again and again they seek to deceive God and themselves by resting on their laurels, that is by attempting to turn a personal relationship which demands grateful response into an established privilege to which they are entitled. But in this way they cut themselves off from the living God. For the Covenant is not meant as an institution which has an independent existence of its own, but as a relationship of dependence in which there is a permanent conversation between God and the people.

By misinterpreting the Covenant or by breaking it altogether it is rendered inoperative. But God's mercy is so great that even then the Covenant is not abolished. Instead of breaking off the relationship he makes a new departure and renews the Covenant.

That is why we hear in the Old Testament of so many different covenants. There is one fundamental covenant-relationship, but this takes many different forms. Thus St Paul when speaking of the characteristics of Israel speaks of covenants in the plural rather than the singular (Rom. 9.4 and Eph. 2.12). In some cases the specific covenants differ in character. It is for example possible to distinguish between the covenant with Noah as a covenant for the sake of the conservation of humanity and the covenant with Abraham as a covenant for the sake of the formation of a holy people. But once we have reached the Sinaitic Covenant, it would seem that there is no place for further covenants except a radically new one such as that of Jeremiah 31. In fact we hear again and again of the making of covenants. The first Sinaitic Covenant (Ex. 19) is re-established soon afterwards (Ex. 34). At the end of the desert journey there is the covenant in the plain of Moab (Deut. 29) and after the entrance into the promised land the covenant at Shechem (Josh. 24). Another covenant is announced to David (II Sam. 7) and confirmed to Solomon (II Chron. 7). Hezekiah (II Chron. 29) makes a special covenant with the Lord and Josiah after having discovered the Book of the Law does the same

(II Kings 23). Finally in the days of Nehemiah after the return from the exile the Levites acting for the whole people make a 'sure covenant' (Neh. 9).

It is clear that these many covenants are not separated acts unrelated to each other. They are rather in the nature of the re-establishment of the true and basic relationship. They are necessary because that relationship is again and again broken. 'Their plurality shows, to what extent the Covenant was only maintained from one side.'[1] In other words it belongs to the very life of the people of God that it must accept again and again to have its life renewed by a new confrontation with its Lord and his holy will.

These great renewals of life cannot take place unless the people turn away from their idolatry and their false security. That is why the new covenants are so often connected with acts of repentance. The second Sinaitic Covenant is preceded by Moses' confession of the sins of the people. Hezekiah and Josiah are found worthy to receive a covenant because they humble themselves before the Lord. The solemn covenant after the return from the Exile can only be concluded after a fast and a penetrating confession of the sins of the past.

The renewal of Israel is the work of God himself. The new departure does not begin with a decision of the leaders to return to religion. It begins with a new encounter with the living God, who does not give up his plan of salvation. God says: 'I will heal their backsliding' (Hos. 14.4). The people's prayer must be: 'Turn thou me, and I shall be turned, for thou art the Lord my God' (Jer. 31.18). It is when the people are once again confronted with their Lord and with his inescapable word of judgment and mercy that they come to realize the nature and depth of their sin.

To repent is to turn about. Renewal is to give up the old

---

[1] Karl Barth, *Kirchliche Dogmatik*, II, 2, 224; cf. *K.D.*, IV, 1, 24.

ways. And what is the old way? The way of rebellion, the way of self-seeking and egocentricity. Fundamentally the one and only sin of Israel is the sin of pride. 'Thou didst trust in thine own beauty' says Ezekiel (16.15). The great tragedy is that when the people are allowed to live in quiet and prosperity they become convinced that they are the architects of their own fate. In the song of Moses we read how the Lord made the people 'ride on the high places of the earth'. But with what result? 'Jeshurun waxed fat and kicked . . . then he forsook God which made him and lightly esteemed the Rock of his salvation' (Deut. 32).

But the deepest tragedy is that the Covenant itself, God's self-giving, becomes a wall of separation between God and man. There is an inveterate tendency to think of God's election as a guarantee, as a policy of insurance, as a right established once and for all. There is a self-glorification, an idolatry of their own spiritual existence which makes the living God superfluous. Why should they bother about the Lord's judgments since they are once and for all the chosen people? Why should they not say as the priests say in the prophecy of Micah: 'Is not the Lord among us? None evil can come upon us' (3.11)? Over against this total misunderstanding of the true meaning of the Covenant the Lord mobilizes prophets. Their first task is to break down this wall of self-satisfied and fundamentally idolatrous piety. They have to make it inescapably clear that the true situation is the reverse of what the religious leaders think. It is not that their election has put them outside the reach of God's judgment; it is rather that judgment begins at the house of God. So they have to proclaim God's wrath upon all who are 'at ease in Zion' (Amos 6.1) and who trust 'in lying words, saying the temple of the Lord, the temple of the Lord, the temple of the Lord' (Jer. 7.4).

The renewal of the Church in the Old Testament is therefore essentially the liberation of the Church out of its self-made prison. Again and again the Church needs to be protected against the downward pull in its own life by which it becomes an aim in itself and ceases to be the obedient servant of its Lord. More dangerous than the worship of all the pagan idols is the self-worship of the chosen people, for that self-worship can so very easily be made to appear as 'the real thing', while in reality it is the exact opposite of God's design.

But the mission of the prophets is not only to pave the way for the renewed acceptance of the Old Covenant. They are at the same time the heralds of a totally new covenant. The three great prophets Isaiah, Jeremiah and Ezekiel announce the day when God will establish a new relationship with man. This will be an 'everlasting' relationship for it will represent God's definitive offer to man. It will be a covenant in the sense that it is a permanent relationship. But it will not be in the nature of a juridical and external link between God and man. Its radically new element will be that it will be a freely accepted spiritual communion.

The basic passage describing this utterly new and unprecedented Covenant is the 31st chapter of Jeremiah. God will write his law in the hearts of men. That means that the law will no longer be a rule of life inscribed on stones and therefore external to men; it will be a law which is so gladly accepted, so gratefully carried out that it becomes part and parcel of the life of men and therefore ceases to be a law. Ezekiel gives us a commentary upon this passage when he speaks of the new spirit which the Lord will give to men, when he takes 'the stony heart out of their flesh and will give them a heart of flesh' (Ezek. 36.26), for that means a heart which will not be obstinate and rebellious, but lets itself be formed and transformed by the Spirit of God.

It is significant that in Ezekiel's prophecy this announcement is followed by the vision of the resurrection of the dry bones. For that vision shows that the renewal of spirit which 'the whole house of Israel' needs is not meant as a mere improvement of their life, but as a total renewal, as a passage from death to life. Moreover the prophet makes it clear that even if the scattered bones are brought together, that is, if all has been done in a human 'organizational' way to renew the life of the people, there is still no breath, no life in the people of God, until God's own breath comes upon it. The New Covenant will consist in an outpouring of the Spirit of God. That Spirit can make the driest bones come alive.

How will this Covenant come into being? It would seem that Deutero-Isaiah in the 'Servant-hymn' in the 42nd chapter has understood that the most radically new element of that Covenant will be that it will not be embodied in a law but in a person. God speaks to the Servant (Isa. 42.6): 'I, Jehovah, have called thee in righteousness, to grasp thee fast by thy hand, and to keep thee, and to set thee for a covenant of the people.' Palestinian Jews before the Christian era[1] and the apostolic Church have interpreted these words in a messianic sense and even though they may also apply to the Israel as a whole, it would seem that this messianic interpretation is justified.

We know how deeply this prophecy, this 'new thing' which God declares (Isa. 42.9) together with other prophecies concerning the Servant of the Lord has influenced the New Testament *kerugma* and how Jesus himself has consciously fulfilled it.[2] And we wonder whether this prophetic

[1] Joachim Jeremias, Kittel, V, 697.

[2] See Joachim Jeremias' convincing answer to the question: Can Jesus have thought of himself as the Servant of the Lord? in Kittel, V, 709-13. Cf. Théo Preiss, *Le Fils de l'Homme*, p. 53.

announcement concerning the servant who is to incarnate in his very life the final Covenant should not be considered alongside of Jeremiah 31 as the background and explanation of Jesus' words that the cup is the New Covenant in his blood.

Thus the sad story of God's generous offer of the Covenant followed by disobedience, by judgment, by renewal, by disobedience again, the unending story of a seemingly vicious circle is not the whole story. The Old Testament itself knows that there is a way out. It points beyond itself to a day when God will create a wholly new situation. Men are not caught within the wheels of a machine which goes eternally through the same motions. For God's creative work goes on. He 'will do a new thing' (Isa. 43.19). There will be a new Adam and a new creation.

These prophetic visions represent the New Testament in the Old Testament. It does not yet become clear just what they mean. Here, if anywhere, we see the truth of Augustine's word, 'What is latent in the Old Testament becomes patent in the New Testament.'

2

THE NEW COVENANT AND
THE NEW CREATION

THE preaching of John the Baptist seems to throw us right back into the Old Testament situation. We hear once again the old prophetic warning and that in its sharpest form. His ultimatum to the unrepentant people is: 'Do not presume to say to yourselves: We have Abraham as our Father; for I tell you, God is able from these stones to raise up children to Abraham' (Matt. 3.9). Is John the Baptist then simply an Old Testament prophet who arrives too late to be of any help? Is he just a relic of the past? No; for his message is dominated by a mysterious announcement. He does not merely say: turn back to God and to the Old Covenant. And he does not only point to a day in the future when the Lord will take the situation in hand. He says: 'Repent, for the kingdom of heaven is at hand.' He announces that God is about to intervene in a new way, for the Kingdom of Heaven means the direct rule of God.

The message which Jesus brings is literally the same. He also proclaims repentance and the nearness of the Kingdom. And at first sight it seems therefore that there is no difference between his preaching and that of the Baptist. But in reality there is a vast difference. For Jesus does not only *announce* the Kingdom. In him the Kingdom is actually *present*. The authority with which he proclaims the new commandments: 'But I say unto you', the divine forgiveness which he brings:

'My son, your sins are forgiven', the casting out of demons and the healing of the sick—all these are signs that in him the Kingdom is really present. It is true that it is not yet present in full visibility—for the Kingdom is not coming with signs to be observed (Luke 17.20) and it is only recognized by those who have eyes to see and ears to hear. It is also true that the old world continues to exist. But a fundamentally new situation has arisen. That situation can be described as the beginning of the fulfilment of the promises which God had made.

The message and ministry of Jesus imply both the New Covenant and the new creation. Schniewind says: 'The significance of this passage [i.e. Jer. 31.31-34] for the whole New Testament, which received its name from these words, cannot be overestimated',[1] and his interpretation of the Sermon on the Mount is so fully convincing because he sees it as the announcement of the New Covenant. Again the miracles of healing are signs of the breaking through of the new creation into the old world.

Jesus refers explicitly to this newness in the sayings concerning the sewing of a piece of cloth on an old garment and the putting of new wine into old wineskins (Mark 2.21, 22 et par.). It should be noticed that the words follow immediately upon the clearly eschatological saying about the bridegroom and the wedding in which Jesus explains that the disciples live joyfully rather than mournfully because the Messiah is among them.[2] In that situation the question

[1] *Die geistliche Erneuerung des Pfarrerstandes*, p. 16.

[2] C. H. Dodd and Joachim Jeremias (Kittel, IV, 1096) consider the passage as a general eschatological rather than as a specific messianic parable. Hoskyns, Schniewind and Kümmel (*Verheissung und Erfüllung*, p. 32 and p. 41) have however given convincing reasons for the messianic interpretation. It represents an indirect witness to Jesus as the Messiah, such as we find several times in the synoptic Gospels.

arises: what is the relation between the new and the old, between that which has come into the world in Jesus himself and the old established order of things. The answer is that the new situation demands new forms of life. It is simply not possible to go on living in the old way when one has come face to face with the Kingdom of God as one meets it in Jesus. The new world is a disruptive element in the old world. The forces of the new age are explosive forces. The new wine will burst the skins.

There remains however a difficult question. Must we then take it that the coming of Jesus is identical with the final arrival of the Kingdom of God? Is the newness which he brings the ultimate renewal? Have the prophecies concerning the new creation now been fulfilled completely and definitely? Has the eschatological promise been realized?

The four passages in the three Synoptic Gospels and in the first Epistle to the Corinthians which describe the Last Supper are specially significant in this connection. For all of them speak of newness, but they speak of it in different ways. Thus St Paul emphasizes the newness of the Covenant which is established by the death of Christ (I Cor. 11.25). In that Covenant the new life is present among us. On the other hand, St Matthew and St Mark[1] simply speak of the Covenant without calling attention to its newness, but they speak in this connection of the newness which is to come, of the new life in the Kingdom of God. For according to them Jesus says: 'I tell you I shall not drink again of the (this) fruit of the vine until that day when I drink it new (with you) in the Kingdom (my Father's Kingdom).'

It is remarkable that we have two versions of St Luke's

[1] The manuscript evidence for reading in Mark 14.24 the *New* Covenant is clearly insufficient. The newest translations have rightly left out the word 'new' in this verse.

account, one which refers to the newness already realized and one which speaks of the newness to be expected in the future. For the manuscripts which belong to the Alexandrian family speak like St Paul of the New Covenant. But the shorter version of Codex D does not refer to the Covenant, but includes this saying of Jesus (22.16): 'I tell you I shall never eat it [i.e. the Passover] again until I eat it new in the Kingdom of God.' In other words we have a group of versions of sayings of Jesus concerning the Last Supper which emphasize the newness already given by his coming and we have others which emphasize the newness which is still to be expected when the Kingdom of God will come in its full glory.

Is there a basic contradiction? Certainly not. For it is quite clear that when Matthew and Mark refer to the Covenant they are specifically thinking of the *New* Covenant of Jer. 31. On the other hand, it is equally clear that St Paul and St Luke (in the Alexandrian version) set the whole story of the Last Supper in an eschatological context and consider the meal as a meal of anticipation or expectation.[1] For all it is true that 'in celebrating the supper, Jesus and his disciples are as it were on the threshold of the new world: already the past event of the Exodus has found its fulfilment, and nevertheless the present and the past will only be fully realized in the Kingdom'.[2] There is the newness which has already come; there is the newness which is yet to come.

These two aspects of the new situation created by the coming of the Messiah are to be found in all New Testament writings. Emphases may differ, but in none is the new merely future or wholly realized.[3] The tension between these

---

[1] I Cor. 11.26 and Luke 22.18.

[2] Théo Preiss in *Theologische Zeitschrift*, 1948, March–April, p. 92.

[3] The two keywords *kainos* and *neos* are both used in the two meanings, although *kainos* has a more specifically eschatological reference.

two aspects of the Gospel is most clearly seen in the Epistles of St Paul. The New Covenant and the new creation are essential elements of his witness.

Writing to the Corinthians (II Cor. 3.3) he describes them as a letter from Christ written, not with ink but with the Spirit of the living God, not on tablets of stone but on tablets of human hearts. That is of course a reminder that the New Covenant prophesied by Jeremiah and Ezekiel is now in force. Again, when in the same epistle he speaks of the new creation in Christ, and says, 'the old has passed away, behold the new has come' (II Cor. 5.17), this is clearly an echo of Isaiah's 'Behold I create a new heaven and a new earth: and the former shall not be remembered, nor come to mind' (Isa. 65.17).

But what exactly does this mean for men? What does St Paul mean by renewal of life?

In the Epistle to the Galatians we read: 'Neither is circumcision anything, nor uncircumcision, but a new creation. Peace and mercy be upon all who walk by this rule, upon the Israel of God' (Gal. 6.15-16). This verse shows that the God who had chosen Israel continues his work. The name 'Israel of God' has been transferred to those who accept and live by God's revelation in Jesus Christ. They are the true successors of the people of the Covenant and inherit the promises made to that people. But there is also a great difference. For a decisive event has taken place. The rule of their life or better the specific criterion (canon) which distinguishes the new people from other men is not the *Torah*, but their place in the new creation.

That means that the coming of Jesus Christ is far more than an important new chapter in the dealings of God with his people; it is nothing less than the breaking in of a new age, of the totally new age represented by the Kingdom of God, the age of the new creation. Thus the words 'new', 'new-ness', 'renewal' are used in the most radical sense. The new-ness of the apostolic witness lies not merely in the fact that it differs from the Old Testament witness; it lies above all in the fact that it proclaims the inauguration of the era of the last days. When we hear of the *new* Jerusalem and of the *new* heaven and the *new* earth, we have to do with the 'last things', with the life of the age to come. For with Christ the Kingdom has entered into this old world. His resurrection is the victory of the new creation over the old and points to the resurrection of all who believe in his name (I Cor. 15). For he is, as it is put in Colossians (1.18), the beginning, that is the beginning of the final age. He is 'the first born from the dead' (1.18), that is the first to have entered fully into the glory of fulfilment. Thus Ignatius does not go beyond the thought of St Paul when he calls Christ 'the new man'.[1]

Now the faithful are invited to share with Christ in this new life. That is the meaning of baptism which makes us participants in the death, but also in the resurrection of Christ and so transplants us into the new life. St Paul says: 'We were buried therefore with him by baptism into death, so that as Christ was raised from the dead by the glory of the Father, we too might walk in newness of life' (Rom. 6.4). But if this is true, a Christian is not simply a person whose life has been renewed in a moral and spiritual sense; a Christian is a person who shares in that total newness of life which is contained in the new creation. He has 'tasted the powers of the age to come' (Heb. 6.5).

Why then does the New Testament contain so many appeals to the Christians to let themselves be renewed? If they *are* new creatures, do they still need renewal? We must

[1]*Ad. Eph.* 20.1.

be particularly careful to do the fullest justice to the biblical teaching on this subject, for, as the whole history of the Church shows, even a slight deviation on this point will have very serious consequences for our view of the situation in which the Church finds itself in this world.

If we look at the passages which speak about newness of life and renewal we find that some of them speak of the new life as an established fact, some of them speak of it as a task to be accomplished and some of them contain these two perspectives together. These last passages show us the way to an understanding of the relationship between the affirmation: 'You are new men' and the exhortation: 'Be renewed.' Thus in I Cor. 5.6-8 the Corinthians are warned to cleanse out the old leaven so that they may be fresh dough, but this exhortation is confirmed by the affirmation that they *are* really unleavened. In other words St Paul says: renew yourself for you *are* new people. Similarly in Colossians (3.9) the imperative, 'Do not lie to one another' is supported by the argument that the Colossians *have* put off the old nature and put on the new nature. But here a further explanation is given namely that this new man *is* being renewed. In other words we have now three statements: the Christian is a new man; he is to seek renewal; he is being renewed. Other passages in the New Testament emphasize one or the other of these three aspects. (See Rom. 7.6; Eph. 4.23; II Cor. 4.16.) Thus it is clear that these three statements are meant as complementary truths.

But how can they be true together? We find the answer in the eschatological character of the newness of life. When we say 'eschatological' we refer to a reality which by its very nature can only be described by seemingly contradictory statements. For we have to do with the presence of a new age in the midst of the old age. And that means that we have to do with a spiritual presence which cannot be adequately described in terms of this world. A passage in Romans (12.2) can help us to understand this. St Paul says: 'Do not be conformed to this age (*aioon*) but be transformed by the renewal of your mind.' The old man is the man who lives according to the ways of this passing age. The new man lives according to the ways of the new age which in one sense has come in Jesus Christ, but in another sense is yet to come. The Christian *is* a new being because he belongs to Christ and to the new age. His newness of life is according to Romans (6.4) the natural consequence of the fact that through his baptism he shares in the death and resurrection of Christ. But this Christian is still surrounded by and involved in the forms of life of the old age. His task is to demonstrate the reality of his new life by a constant struggle against the hold of the old age upon him and to conform himself increasingly to the ways of the new age. In this he is assisted by the Holy Spirit so that (as St Paul puts it in II Cor. 4.16) 'our inner nature is being renewed every day'. In other words there is no fundamental contradiction. Althaus puts it very clearly: 'Precisely because the Christian belongs with Christ to the new age, he must struggle within the old age against the old age. . . . The basis of his struggle is the victory but the victory is only real in his struggle.'[1]

This then is the paradoxical nature of the new life in Christ. It is characterized by an 'already' and a 'not yet'. In Christ the Christian is *already* the new man. But he is *not yet* transplanted into the Kingdom. He *has* died, but his new life is still *hid* with Christ in God (Col. 3.3). He lives on the frontier of two worlds which are in conflict with each other. But in this dangerous situation he is not left to himself. For Christ is at work in renewing him. According to Ephesians

[1] See Althaus in *N.T.Deutsch. Commentary on Romans*, p. 53.

(4.23) this renewal is at the same time a constant rejuvenation. St Chrysostom[1] remarks concerning the key-word (*ananeousthai*) of this verse: that it 'means that something old is renewed (rejuvenated) and thus becomes different. That which is *neos* is strong. It has no wrinkle.'

What does this mean for the Church? We will attempt to group the answer of the New Testament under ten headings.

1. *The new people of God represents the new humanity inaugurated by the new man Jesus Christ.*

In the Epistle to the Ephesians (2.14-15) we read that Christ has broken down the dividing wall separating the Gentiles from the Jews, in order to 'create in himself one new man in place of two'. What this means is well expressed by Stauffer: 'The Church is the new humanity, the pioneer of which is Jesus Christ. It is the new man. The new situation of the world created by the unique event of the coming of Christ, becomes in the present age a positive reality only in the form of the Church. And in the Church it is realized only in so far as the Church takes the new situation seriously in its faith, its attitude, its action.'[2]

In the first chapter of Colossians (vv. 17-19) we find a similar affirmation. It is clear that the two statements that Christ is the Head of the Church and that he is the beginning, the first born from the dead, are related. Moffatt gives therefore certainly the true sense of the passage in translating: 'He is the head of the Body, that is of the church, in virtue of his primacy as the first to be born from the dead'.[3] In other words the new man Christ, the new creation and the Church are inextricably bound together.

The same truth is expressed in the affirmation that the

[1] Quoted in Kittel, IV, 904.   [2] Kittel, II, 438.
[3] Similarly M. Dibelius in *Handbuch zum N.T.*

distinctive characteristic of the Church is that the Holy Spirit is poured out upon it. For the Holy Spirit is (in the words of C. H. Dodd) 'evidence of the dawn of the new age'.[1] That is why it is called 'a first fruit' (Rom. 8.23) or an 'earnest', that is a first payment or instalment of our inheritance (Eph. 1.14). The pouring out of the Spirit upon the new people is, according to Joel's prophecy (2.28), an event which takes place 'in the last days'. The Spirit is therefore also the power of the new age which works renewal and transformation within the old age. Our renewal is renewal in the Spirit (Titus 3.5). The new life is life of the Spirit (Rom. 7.6). It is the Spirit which continues to build the Church. Our *koinonia* or fellowship is 'the fellowship of the Spirit' (Phil. 2.1). The Church is a spiritual house, that is to say a house built and rebuilt by the Holy Spirit (I Peter 2.5). All these statements to which many could be added make it very clear that the Church is a radically new fellowship. It is, as the report on the main theme of the Evanston Assembly puts it: 'God's new creation, united to Christ as the body to the head, filled and quickened by his Spirit, God's Holy Temple.'

2. *The new people live however in the dispensation in which the forces of the old age are still active and in which the Kingdom of God is still the object of faith and hope.*

The new people live still in a world which has not yet been renewed. It has not yet reached its destination. That destination is the Kingdom which has been present among us in Christ, but is yet to be manifested in its glory. The Church is not the Kingdom. It expects the Kingdom and preaches the gospel of the Kingdom. The new Jerusalem is still above (Gal. 4.26). Since Christ has appeared, it can be said that we have 'come to' the heavenly Jerusalem (Heb.

---

[1] *The Apostolic Preaching and its Developments*, p. 138.

12.22), but since the total renewal has not yet taken place we are still in the situation in which we have no lasting city and seek the city which is to come (Heb. 13.14).

The new people is therefore a pilgrim-people. As the report on the main theme of the Evanston Assembly puts it: 'It is of its very nature that its members should know themselves to be strangers and pilgrims on the earth, pressing on towards the moment at which the Lord who died and rose again will confront them in his power and glory?'

When the Church calls itself the *Ecclesia*, it emphasizes that it is a people, the people of God. When it calls itself a *paroikia* (as in I Peter 1.17; 2.11 and in our word 'parish') it emphasizes that this people is living in this world as in a foreign country because its members belong as citizens to the Kingdom which is yet to come.[1]

The Church lives therefore by faith and not by sight, with the certain hope and expectation that the Kingdom for the coming of which it prays, will be brought in at God's appointed time.

3. *The new people is constantly under the pressure of the forces of the old age, which penetrate into its life. It needs therefore constantly renewal of life.*

The powers which dominate the present, that is the old, age are in principle overcome in the victory of Christ, but they are still active and do not only operate outside the life of the people of God, but also in its midst. This is made specially clear in the parable of the tares. The enemy, that is Satan, has sown weeds among the wheat. Schniewind remarks: 'Where God sows, the devil also sows.'[2] And there will be no clear-cut separation between the wheat and the

---

[1] See K. L. Schmidt in Kittel, V, 850.
[2] *Das Neue Testament Deutsch*, Matt. 13.24-30.

weeds until the day of the harvest, that is the last judgment. In this world the people will always be a 'mixed company'. The membership of the people here on earth is not exactly the same as the citizenship of the new Jerusalem.

The Church without spot or wrinkle (Eph. 5.27) which is a 'pure bride' (II Cor. 11.2) is the ultimate goal,[1] which will only be realized at the *parousia*.[2] St Augustine says: 'As long as she is here, the whole Church prays: Forgive us our sins. Thus she is here not without spot or wrinkle, but through that, which she has received, she is brought to that glory and perfection, which does not exist here.'[3]

Does that mean that the new people must passively accept its imperfections and not react against the invasion of the old age into its life? Surely not. If it realizes the great contradiction between its calling and the reality of its life, it will pray constantly for the renewal of its life. Knowing that Christ himself cleanses it, it will seek to cleanse itself.

There is an important analogy between the renewal and the edification of the Church. The Church is the house, the building built by God. It is the old 'dwelling of David' (Acts 15.16) which has been rebuilt. It needs constant building up (Eph. 4.12; 4.16). *Ecclesia edificanda quia aedificata*. Exactly in the same way the new people made new by God needs renewal. *Ecclesia renovanda quia renovata*.

4. *In this respect the new people of God is in the same situation as the people of the Old Covenant.*

There are many differences between the old and the new people of God. But with respect to this need for renewal they

---

[1] *Ultimus finis*. St Thomas, quoted in de Lubac, *Méditation sur l'Église*, p. 91.

[2] The verb *paristemi* used in both passages is generally used in an eschatological context.

[3] Quoted by Grosche, *Pilgernde Kirche*, p. 66.

are in the same situation. For it would be a very unbiblical conception of the history of the old and new Israel to distinguish them as the people who had to live in insecurity and the people who live in security or as the people who were confronted with God's judgment and the people who are no longer concerned with that judgment.

Both the old and the new Israel live under the shadow of the judgment and in the sun of the grace of God. Both are called to newness of life. Origen says graphically of the two Testaments: 'They have not the same age, but their object is the same newness.'[1] There is a profound continuity in the dealings of God with his people.

5. *The new people of God must therefore take to heart the solemn warnings addressed to the people of Israel in the Old Testament.*

The people of the New Covenant cannot afford to look down upon the people of the Old Covenant or to consider the events of the history of Israel as a matter of merely historical interest. This is made very clear by St Paul in the tenth chapter of the Corinthians (vv. 1-13). St Paul teaches that the spiritual and sacramental gifts which the people in the desert received were fundamentally the same as those which have been granted to the new people, but that in spite of this fact they rebelled against God and were consequently rejected. Now this is a 'type' for us (verse 6). These things happened 'typically' and were written down for our instruction (verse 11). That is to say these events are not events that happened long ago and far away. They belong to the experience of the people of God; they are *our* history and they must live in our hearts and minds as most relevant warnings and examples.

In the third and fourth chapters of the Epistle to the

[1] Quoted by Florovsky, *La Sainte Église Universelle*, p. 15.

Hebrews we find exactly the same approach. Again the new people are confronted with the history of the old people and again it is the rebellion in the desert which must warn the new Israel. For both the old and the new Israel live by a promise of God, both are in danger of provoking God, both may fail to enter his 'rest', the sabbath-rest of the Kingdom. The situations are identical except in one crucial respect. The new Israel has a great high-priest who, though he is Son of God, is able to sympathize with the weaknesses of the people and therefore to support them in their struggles.

The Epistle of Jude is a particularly strong example of the relevance of the judgments executed on the people of the Old Covenant, for that epistle is wholly dominated by reminders of the awful results of its rebellions. Cain, Sodom and Gomorrah, Balaam, Korah, the disobedience in the desert—all these are used as illustrations of God's dealings with his people and as examples of the danger in which the new people find themselves. But the epistle closes with the doxology: 'To him who is able to keep you from falling.' If the Church counts on him and 'keeps itself in the love of God', it need not fear.

6. *Judgment begins at the House of God*

It is not merely that the people are to count with the general judgment of God which will embrace all humanity. Precisely because they are God's special people (I Peter 2.9) they are to be judged in a special way.

'Judgment begins at the House of God' (I Peter 4.17). What does this mean? It is clear that the House of God is the Church. Now the verse is obviously related to Jeremiah 25.29 where we read: 'I begin to work evil at the city which is called by my name.' This expresses a truth which permeates the whole Old Testament. Because God has chosen Israel it is called to be a holy nation, but this implies that God does not allow Israel to go its own way. Through his judgments he calls it back to himself. His judgments are the necessary counterpart of his election of the people. Karl Barth puts it this way: 'By binding himself to Israel, God binds Israel to himself and by binding Israel to himself, he becomes for it the fire which is not extinguished and the flame of which is again nothing else than the flame of his love.'[1]

Now in this respect the new people is in the same situation as the old people. The New Covenant does not mean that the love of God comes in the place of his holiness. On the contrary the cross has made it even more clear that his love is a holy love and that his mercy and his judgment are inseparable. The difference between the new and the old is however that God now offers an even greater salvation (Heb. 2.3). The warning is all the more serious and solemn since it comes to those 'upon whom the end of the ages has come' (I Cor. 10.11). If the people who had the Covenant of Moses were judged, how much more will this be true of the people who have the Covenant of the Son of God (Heb. 10.29).

The nature of the judgment is made clear by St Paul in I Corinthians 11.32: 'When we (the Christians) are judged by the Lord, we are chastened, so that we may not be condemned along with the world.' This chastening (*paideuein*) belongs to the *paideia kuriou*, the divine pedagogy, which is further described in Hebrews 12. The Lord disciplines (again *paideuein*) him whom he loves. His pedagogy is not a pedagogy of moral exhortation, not a pedagogy of inflicting punishment to frighten the evil-doer. It is the way of the loving father. In fact his discipline shows that he treats his people as sons. For his purpose is their good which is that they may share in his holiness.

[1] *Kirchliche Dogmatik*, II, 1, 412.

Now these judgments are not only an individual matter. They concern the people, the House of God. It is to the *Church* of Laodicea that the words are spoken: 'Those whom I love, I reprove and chasten; so be zealous and repent' (Rev. 3.19).

7. *The new people is constantly placed before the choice between 'apostasy' and 'hypomone'.*

We read in Luke 8.13 that there are people who receive the word with joy, but who, since they have no root, believe for a while and in time of temptation fall away or more literally 'apostatize'. Now this danger of apostasy, of denial of the Lord is a constant danger for the new people as it was for the old.[1] Even those who have become partakers of the Holy Spirit and have tasted the goodness of the Word of God and the powers of the age to come can commit apostasy (Heb. 6.5-6). The apostolic Church is fully aware that the astounding gifts which it has received are not in the nature of an insurance policy against apostasy. We find therefore the warnings against such falling away in all parts of the New Testament. In the synoptic Gospels we have them in the announcement of the eschatological events in Mark 13.6, 21 or Matthew 24.5, 11 and in the parable of the foolish virgins. In the letters to the seven churches in the Book of Revelation the theme of faithfulness versus apostasy is the *Leitmotif.* And both St Paul and St John announce that the Anti-Christ, who is the tempter (II John 7), will seek to lead the people astray from within the Church (I John 2.18, 19 and II Thess. 2.3-4). That the last named passage concerning 'the son of perdition' is to be understood as referring to a

[1] In addition to *aphistemi* and 'apostasy' the words for 'denying', 'leading astray' and 'tempting' should be kept in mind here.

'domestic enemy'[1] and not to an enemy from without is indicated by the use of the word 'apostasy', for that word is only used for the falling away of those who have belonged to the community of the faithful.[2]

Now this would be an unbearable message if it were not counterbalanced and even overshadowed by the promise that in this terrible insecurity the people of God may count on the powerful help of God himself. God is the God of *hypomone* (Rom. 15.5). That word is hard to translate because of its rich content. It means the divine gift of stead-fast endurance and patience, but also active resistance against the temptation of apostasy. The well-known verses at the beginning of Hebrews 12 have this *hypomone* as their central theme. 'Let us run with perseverance (*hypomone*) the race . . . looking to Jesus who . . . endured (*hypomenein*) the cross . . . consider him who endured (*hypomenein*) . . .' (1-3). In Mark 13.13 we read that those who will endure (*hypomone*) till the end will be saved. And in the Book of Revelation *hypomone* is one of the great keywords and we hear in the midst of the noise of the cosmic battle the war-cry: 'Here is the *hypomone* of the saints' (14.12; cf. 13.10), that is of the true Church of God.

8. *The forces of this (old) age will not prevail against the people of God.*

It is certain that in the great battle between Christ and the adversary Christ will be victorious, for he has already achieved victory. And this implies that the people which belong to him cannot be annihilated. There will always be a

---

[1] Calvin on II Thess. 2.4.

[2] See Kittel, I, 510. Whether the appearance of the Anti-Christ 'in the temple' also underlines that apostasy will take place *within* the Church remains uncertain. St Augustine leaves the question open (*De Civ. Dei*, 20, 19).

people of God. His sheep 'shall never perish' and no one shall snatch them out of his hand (John 10.28). For he will be always with them to the close of the age (Matt. 28.20).

The forces of the old age will do everything to lead astray the elect, but they will ultimately fail because God will maintain the faith of the saints. The attempt to lead astray, 'if possible', the elect (Mark 13.22) is bound to fail.[1] That is also implied in the promise: 'Fear not, little flock, for it is your Father's good pleasure to give you the kingdom' (Luke 12.32). And whatever the exact significance of the expression 'the gates of Hades' may be,[2] it is clear that Matt. 16.18 means that the powers of darkness and death shall not prevail against the messianic community created by and united to Jesus Christ.

9. *But no member, no section, no institution forming part of the life of the people, is exempt from the judgment of God.*

God's firm foundation stands, but on that foundation it is written: the Lord knows those who are his (II Tim. 2.19). Therein lies the great paradox of the New Testament conception of the Church. The Church cannot fail, but only God knows who belongs to it and who does not. For, as St Augustine puts it, God's 'will was to keep it unknown, who belongs to the devil and who does not. For this is hidden in the present age, since it is uncertain whether he that seems to stand will fall and whether he that seems to fall will rise again.'[3] No member of the Church, no part of the Church, no institution or office within it can take it for granted that

---

[1] Kittel, IV, 193; cf. verse 22 with verse 20. Schniewind translates 'if it were possible'.

[2] Cf. the various possible interpretations mentioned by Oscar Cullmann in *Peter—Disciple, Apostle, Martyr*, p. 201.

[3] *De Civitate Dei*, XX, 7.

it is of the true Church. No one can rest on his laurels. No one can afford to neglect the warnings against apostasy. However improbable it may seem, salt can lose its saltness. It is significant that this warning concerning the loss of one's identity and integrity as a Christian is addressed to the disciples themselves (Matt. 5.13; Mark 9.50). Again the branch which has belonged to the vine can fail to bear fruit, be cast away and wither. William Temple comments: 'There is a profound mystery of iniquity here. It is possible to be genuinely drawn to the Lord, to follow his call, to be of his company, and still bear no fruit.'[1]

And this situation is not only the situation of each individual, it is also the situation of the Christians in their common life in the Church. In the eleventh chapter of Romans St Paul speaks to the Gentile Christians as a body when he says: 'Do not become proud, but stand in awe. For if God did not spare the natural branches, neither will he spare you. Note then the kindness and severity of God: severity towards those who have fallen, but God's kindness to you, provided you continue in his kindness; otherwise you too will be cut off' (vv. 20-22). Karl Barth comments: 'If God has done this to the natural branch, to his people Israel, then he will, if Israel's unbelief should re-appear in the Church, have the power and the will to do the same thing to the Church. . . . It would come automatically under the same judgment, under which it sees Israel standing. No, a more severe judgment, for it would not be in the same situation as the Jews, but in a worse situation, since it would be without the promise given to the Jews, as it does not belong to the natural branch.'[2]

And so we read in the Book of Revelation that the Lord

[1] *Readings in St John's Gospel*, II, 255.
[2] *Kirchliche Dogmatik*, II, 2, 321.

of the Church says to the Church of Ephesus, a church which had shown endurance, but which had abandoned its first love, that, unless it should repent, its lampstand will be removed from its place, that is to say that it will cease to be a Church of Christ (Rev. 2.5).

10. *The whole Church is therefore called to repentance and renewal of life.*

The need of the whole Church for repentance and renewal is most clearly shown in the second and third chapters of the Book of Revelation. It has often been pointed out that the seven churches to whom the letters are addressed represented the most flourishing part of the Church at that time. But more important is that according to the symbolic language of the author the seven churches clearly represent the Church as a whole. For seven is the figure of totality.[1] In these letters the whole Church is addressed. This is underlined by the fact that each letter is concluded by the solemn warning: 'He who has an ear, let him hear what the Spirit says to the churches.' The warning and promise received by each church is meant to be overheard and passed on by the other churches and so to reach the whole Church.[2]

Now it is significant that five of the seven letters are in the nature of calls to repentance. For that means that the Church as such is called to live the life of *metanoia*, of constant readiness to turn away from the path of this world and to let itself be renewed. And once again it is made clear that renewal means living by the power of the new age. In the letter to

[1] See Rengstorf in Kittel, II, 629.

[2] That the whole Church is meant is furthermore illustrated by the fact that in Rev. 2.7 the Alexandrian Codex reads: 'what the Spirit says to the *seven* churches'. Cf. Beda Venerabilis: The seven churches 'are figures of the whole sevenfold Church'.

the Church in Sardis repentance is identified with awakening (3.2 and 3.3). To be awake is to be ready for the Day of the Lord. 'Lo, I am coming like a thief. Blessed is he who is awake' (Rev. 16.15).

The churches are called to remember from what they have fallen (2.5) or what they have received and heard (3.3). That is to say they are to realize again that they represent the new creation. If they do, if they turn resolutely away from the old age, then they will receive the new name (2.17 and 3.12) and be counted as belonging to the new Jerusalem (3.12). Such a *metanoia* is in this world never a completed process; it is to be actualized and implemented every day anew.

3

OLD AND NEW IN THE EARLY CHURCH

THE Church of the first centuries could not avoid facing the problem of the relation between the old and the new in the life of the Church. On the one hand it had a strong consciousness of representing the new humanity. Harnack[1] has written an impressive chapter on this subject and shown how much this message of the emergence of a radically new people has meant for the mission and the expansion of the Church in a tired and decadent civilization. On the other hand the Church considered itself as the only true custodian of the ancient heritage of Israel and found in this inheritance another powerful apologetic argument. Thus it is not astonishing that antiquity and newness appear side by side as essential elements of the faith and life of the Church.

Our purpose in this lecture is to illustrate this tension between the two perspectives and to ask how far the early Church remained faithful to the New Testament teaching concerning renewal.

We will first hear some voices which emphasize strongly that the Church stands for antiquity.

There were two very strong reasons why the spokesmen of the Church emphasized that Christianity had a venerable

[1] *Mission und Ausbreitung*, Chapter on 'Die Botschaft von dem neuen Volke'.

past. The first is that the Gnostics and Marcion sought to construct theological systems in which the New Testament was completely divorced from the Old Testament. It was therefore indispensable to prove the fundamental cohesion of the two covenants. The second reason was the affirmation constantly made by pagan writers that the Christian message was a new-fangled product of the imagination which was not supported by the ancient wisdom of the human race. This accusation of which we find echoes in nearly all authors who expressed themselves on the subject, is clearly formulated by Celsus, the pagan philosopher whom Origen made famous by his answer. He asks why men should exchange their religion consecrated by its antiquity for this faith which has arisen so recently. It is not long ago that Christianity has appeared in the world. What an idea to seek to make this new creed into a world faith! Why should God have waited so long before revealing the way of wisdom and virtue to mankind? Christians are in fact introducing a new error, a new superstition.[1]

It is not surprising that in the face of this challenge Christian preachers and writers emphasized that Christianity had a respectable genealogy. The *Epistle of Barnabas* states that, while God gave the Covenant to the people of Israel, they were not worthy to receive it and that in view of old Israel's apostasy the Christians are the true people of inheritance and of the Covenant (chapter 14). Justin says bluntly: 'we are the true Israelitic race' (*Dial.* 135), 'the true spiritual Israel and descendants of Judah, Jacob, Isaac and Abraham' (*Dial.* 11).

And these ancestors are really 'more ancient than all those who are esteemed philosophers' (*Dial.* 7). This point is confirmed by Origen against Celsus. It is also for this reason that Tertullian can exclaim: 'Your history only goes back to

[1] Karl von Hase, *Kirchengeschichte*, I, pp. 242-5.

the Assyrians; ours is the history from the beginning of the world.'[1]

It is therefore underlined that the Church is extremely old. In the *Shepherd of Hermas* (*Vis.* II, 4) the Church is portrayed as an old lady and it is explained that she is old because she was created before all things. The so-called second letter of Clement speaks of the Church created before the sun and the moon (14.1). Origen believes also that the first foundations of the Church have been laid from the very beginning, that is the creation (*In Cant. Comm.*).[2] And the *Epistle to Diognetus* speaks of Christ in the following striking phrase: 'He, who was from the beginning who appeared new and was found to be old, and is ever born young in the hearts of the saints' (11.4).

Eusebius of Caesarea struggles with this problem at the beginning of his *Church History* (I, 4). He writes as an apologist and his purpose is to show that Christianity is not something new and strange. It is true that a 'new people' has come on the scene. But the Christian way of life is not a recent invention. It has been known since the creation of men. For there have been men in Israel from the days of Noah and Abraham who have lived according to the divine precepts and who have known Christ. And it is this religion, the most ancient of all, which is contained in the Christian message. In these pages of Eusebius the emphasis is so definitely on antiquity that the newness of the gospel is almost obscured.

Must we then conclude that the early Church does not really take the newness of the gospel seriously? No. There lives in it also a grateful amazement about the new initiative which God has taken. The apologetic emphasis on the antiquity of the Christian faith cannot altogether suppress the

[1] Quoted by Harnack, *Mission und Ausbreitung*, p. 268.
[2] Quoted in de Lubac, *Méditation sur l'Église*, p. 49.

sense of newness. And it would seem that the joyful affirmations concerning that newness have a spontaneity such as is not found in the same way in the purely apologetic developments.

Thus Ignatius writes to the Ephesians: 'A star shone in heaven brighter than all the stars. Its light was indescribable and its novelty caused amazement. The rest of the stars, along with the sun and the moon, formed a ring around it; yet it outshone them all, and there was bewilderment whence this unique novelty had arisen. As a result all magic lost its power and all witchcraft ceased. Ignorance was done away with, and the ancient kingdom (of evil) was utterly destroyed, for God was revealing himself as a man, to bring newness of eternal life' (*Eph.* 19.2-3).[1] And from Hippolytus we have this strong statement in a Syrian fragment of an Easter Homily:[2] 'That which has never belonged to the ordinary mysteries, is something new. Or can you pretend that such things have happened before Christ came? You cannot. Now when such things have happened first through Christ, then this is a new mystery: new because of the new church, the new salvation, the new Kingdom, for your sake, since you have been saved in a new way. Your salvation is new because you have been saved in this new manner through the cross and the nails of God.'

Irenaeus says that all things entered upon a new phase when Christ came in the flesh. 'And therefore men were taught to worship God in a new way, but not another God' (III, 10, 2). His purpose is to defend the unity of the two Testaments against Marcion and in doing so he has to show that there is a real continuity as between the old and the new

---

[1] Translation Cyril C. Richardson in *Early Christian Fathers* (Library of Christian Classics).

[2] Quoted by Prümm, *Christentum als Neuheitserlebnis*, p. 468.

Israel. He must therefore emphasize that the gospel is part of a plan of salvation which has a long history. But he does not sacrifice the new to the old. He asks (*Adversus Haereses* II, 34): 'What then did the Lord bring to us by his advent?' And he answers in a magnificent phrase: 'Know ye that he brought all (possible) newness by bringing himself' (*Cognoscite, quoniam omnem novitatem attulit semet ipsum afferens*). He adds that it is like the coming of a long expected king. When he finally comes, men do not ask: has he brought any new thing? For the king is himself the new gift.

Origen, who has such a very strong sense of the unity and continuity of the plan of salvation, can nevertheless also speak with conviction about the new beginning which God has made. He says: 'The Lord has come in the evening of a world in decline, which had nearly finished its course. But through his coming, he, who is the sun of righteousness, has refashioned a new day for those who believe. Since he has illuminated the world with a new light of knowledge, he has created his day in the morning' (*Hom. on Exodus* VII).

It is therefore not surprising that the Christians called themselves 'the new people'. In the New Testament the conception of the Church as the new people is implied;[1] it becomes explicit in the *Epistle of Barnabas* (5.7 and 7.5) and is then used again and again, e.g. by Aristides, the *Epistle to Diognetus*, and Clement of Alexandria. This expression contains the dialectical situation of the Church: its consciousness of being a coherent unit, of being the legitimate heir of Israel, and yet of being something unprecedented. As a new people the Christians are different from both the Greeks and the Jews. The *Praedicatio Petri* (which dates from the beginning of the second century) explains the New Covenant in this manner: 'The way of the Greeks and the Jews is old.

[1] See especially I Peter 2.9-10.

But you are those who worship (God) anew in the third manner, the Christians.'[1] Now in this respect the conception which the Christians had of their Church and the opinion of the pagan world coincided, for Tertullian reports at the end of the second century that the pagans in the circus of Carthage used this battle-cry against the Christians: *Usque quo genus tertium?* (How long must we stand this third race?). And soon afterwards we find the Christians using this invective as a title of honour. An African Christian writes: 'we are the third race'[2] and confirms in this way that the early Church realized that in the new people a completely new force had invaded the life of the world.

★   ★   ★

There can therefore be no doubt that the early Church understood its own existence as the existence of a new creation. We must however ask in how far that new creation was understood in the same sense as in the New Testament. And our first question must be: do we find in the early Church that same conception of newness as the eschatological gift which we find in the New Testament and which is expressed in the tension between the indicative: 'you are new' and the imperative 'be renewed'?

In Irenaeus we find indeed the same dialectical conception of the present and the future newness which is to be found in St Paul. Christ has brought newness of life (IV, 34, 1). The New Covenant renovates man (III, 11, 8). The Holy Spirit renews men from their old ways into the newness of Christ (III, 17, 1). But the full renewal belongs to the eschatological future. The pattern of this world will pass away

---

[1] See Harnack, *Mission und Ausbreitung*, pp. 243 and 265; and Oepke, *Das neue Gottesvolk*, pp. 266-7.

[2] *De Pascha Computus*, Harnack, op. cit., p. 246.

and a new order will come, in which man is made new in such a manner that he will always remain new (V, 36, 1).

Origen's position is hard to define. For on the one hand his theology is strongly eschatological. There are not two peoples but three: Israel, the Church and the Assembly of the Kingdom of God.[1] He preaches that we must never be silent concerning the last things and the end of the world.[2] But when it comes to defend the Christian Church against Celsus the eschatological perspective is greatly weakened. In the well-known passage in which the Christian churches are compared with the non-Christian communities we find a curious mixture of eschatology and moralism. On the one hand the Christian churches are still described as colonies (*paroikia*) of strangers on earth; on the other hand the difference between the Christians and the pagans is not defined in terms of the old and the new age, but in terms of lesser or greater progress in virtue.[3] And this is not wholly due to the apologetic purpose, for in the *Homilies on Jeremiah*[4] we find a passage which links that same idea of progress with the new creation and speaks of a *gradual* improvement of the new creature. Thus Origen leaves us in spite of the wealth of his penetrating exegetical remarks with a feeling of uncertainty as to his understanding of renewal.

In lesser writers this moralism comes out much more crudely. The 'new law' tends to take the place of the new creation. Bishop Nygren[5] has shown that the expression 'the new law' does not necessarily have a legalistic and moralistic connotation, for it can be used in the sense of the New

[1] de Lubac in the Introduction of *Origene: Homélies sur l'Exode* (Sources Chrétiennes), p. 32.

[2] Ibid., p. 218.   [3] *Contra Celsum*, III, 29-30.

[4] See *Enchiridion Patristicum*, no. 487: '*ut fiat nova creatura melior*'.

[5] *Agape and Eros*, 1953 edition, p. 273.

Covenant. But it is clear that in the *Epistle of Barnabas* and in the *Shepherd of Hermas*[1] and later in Tertullian the 'nomos-type' dominates and that the eschatological conception of renewal as radical and total *metanoia* is replaced by the relative concept of fulfilling new moral commandments. In this respect the situation is therefore that two concepts of renewal, the biblical one and the moralistic one, operate in the Church and in its theology at one and the same time.

★   ★   ★

Our next question is whether we find in the early Church that same sense of standing under the judgment of God which expresses itself in the application of the divine warnings contained in the Old Testament to the new people of God.

There are two reasons why the Church of the early centuries does not apply these warnings to its own life to the same extent as the Church of the apostolic age.

The first has to do with the development of the conception of the Church. Very soon after the apostolic period it becomes customary to speak of the Church in such terms that the difference between it and the Kingdom of God is obscured. The Church is described as pre-existent. Clement's Second Letter speaks of 'the first Church, the spiritual one, which was created before the sun and the moon' which 'existed from the beginning' (ch. 14). Gustave Bardy comments that when the Church is thus conceived in a context of images and symbols it loses its historical reality.[2] Now this danger appears in various forms in the writings of many of the church fathers. Again and again the Church is

---

[1] See Kittel, IV, 1003.
[2] *La Théologie de l'Église de S. Clément de Rome à S. Irénée*, p. 165.

identified with the New Jerusalem.[1] It is well known how in the thought of St Augustine the conception of the Church oscillates between two poles, so that in certain passages we find him speaking of the Church as practically identical with the Kingdom of God,[2] while in other passages he calls such an identification an insane presumption;[3] or that he speaks at one time of the present Church as having no spot or wrinkle and at other times states clearly that this qualification can only be applied to the Church in heaven.[4] Now it is inevitable that when the word 'church' cannot be used without calling to mind the pure, spiritual, otherworldly Church it becomes difficult or even impossible to apply to it the warnings given to the people of Israel. To say of this Church that it stands under the judgment of God would in this context sound as a *contradictio in terminis*.

Now this difficulty is increased by the fact that there appears in the early Church a tendency to interpret the formation of the new people of God in such a way that the old people has never been a true people of God. There is, as Harnack puts it, a growing anti-Judaism[5] and the teaching contained in the chapters nine to eleven of the Epistle to the Romans is largely forgotten. The *Epistle of Barnabas* (4.7-8;

[1] K. L. Schmidt in *Die Polis in Kirche und Welt*, gives many examples. See especially pp. 59 and 67.

[2] *De Civitate Dei*, XX, 9.

[3] *De Virgin.*, 24. This uncertainty has never been resolved in Roman Catholic theology. See the discussion between Vosnier and Grosche in Grosche, *Pilgernde Kirche*, pp. 41 ff. Cf. de Lubac, *Méditation sur l'Église*, p. 51.

[4] In his *Retractationes* Augustine says that where he has spoken of the Church as being without spot or wrinkle this must not be understood as applying to the Church as it is, but as it will be. For now the whole Church must say every day: Forgive us our debts.

[5] *Mission und Ausbreitung*, p. 68. Fully described in Oepke, *Das Neue Volk Gottes*, pp. 281 ff. See also p. 268.

10.12; 13.1) gives us to understand that Israel never had any right to the Covenant and that the Covenant is meant for Christians alone. And in various ways this thought reappears in later authors, in a number of cases combined with an Anti-Semitism in which non-theological factors play a considerable role. Now it is clear that in such a conception of the history of Israel the Old Testament warnings and exhortations to the people are increasingly considered as further proofs of the fundamental inability of the Jews to understand the will of God, rather than as warnings which are just as relevant for the life of the new people as for the old. There appears the danger that the new people is so certain that it is the chosen people that it may repeat the very sin of self-righteousness which became the reason for the rejection of the old people.

This makes it all the more important that from some of the church fathers we hear echoes of the New Testament teaching concerning the relevance of the warnings of the Old Testament to the new people of God. For this means that in spite of the counter-currents which we have just mentioned the consciousness that judgment begins at the House of God has not disappeared altogether.

In the first *Epistle of Clement* (ch. 8 and 9) the Church of Corinth is reminded that it should repent and this is done on the basis of Ezekiel's words concerning the needed repentance of 'the house of Israel'. The implication is clearly that repentance is not merely an individual matter, but that it concerns the whole Church at Corinth.

Even the *Epistle of Barnabas* with its dangerous tendency to divorce the new people completely from the old, brings out that the new people must heed the ancient warnings. It says: 'And all the more attend to this, my brethren, when you reflect and behold, that after so great signs and wonders were wrought in Israel, they were thus (at length) abandoned. Let us beware lest we be found (fulfilling that saying), as it is written: Many are called, but few are chosen' (*Barn.* 4.14). This means surely that according to Barnabas the new people now stands under that special judgment of God under which the old people had lived before the coming of Christ.

The *Shepherd of Hermas* in which the images and symbols fluctuate in such a disconcerting manner, speaks of the testing of the tower, which is the Church, but in the further development the application is individual rather than collective (IX, 5, 6-7).

In the writings of Irenaeus of Lyons we find clear confirmation that the teaching of St Paul and of the Epistle to the Hebrews on this subject is not forgotten. Irenaeus teaches consistently that the God of the Old and the God of the New Covenant are one and the same God. It is this God, the Father of our Lord and the God of the prophets, who is both Judge and Saviour, who calls the unworthy, but examines those who are called in order to ascertain whether they have put on the garment fit and proper for the marriage of his Son. Therefore the new people must be watchful, for 'as in the former covenant with many of them he was not well pleased, so also it is the case here that many are called but few are chosen' (IV, 36, 6).

Irenaeus takes St Paul's exhortation in I Corinthians 10 very seriously and quotes more than once the keywords of that passage that these things were written down 'for our instruction'. He is also a faithful follower of the apostles in that he says: do not blame the old people, but fear lest perchance we be shut out of God's Kingdom (IV, 27, 2). We of the present time are also 'inquired into'. Just as the unrighteous perished then, so it is now. These things are not said to those without, but to us. A little leaven leaveneth the whole lump (IV, 27, 3,4). The implication is clearly: people of God, do not boast, but fear the Lord and repent.

That Irenaeus is not merely writing down some pious reflections but means what he says becomes clear in another passage (IV, 26, 3-4). Here the Old Testament warning is applied to the church leaders, the 'presbyters'. The (apocryphal) story of Daniel and the elders who had falsely accused Susannah, is used to show that leaders who are 'puffed with the pride of holding the chief seat' will be 'convicted by the Word'. The faithful must keep aloof from these and only adhere to those who holding to the doctrine of the apostles and while having the priesthood, display sound speech and blameless conduct. It would seem to follow that where there is self-seeking, pride and no repentance, there is no true Church.

It is an impressive fact that Origen who has an extremely 'high', spiritualized, conception of the Church has nevertheless several passages in which the danger of collective apostasy of the new people of God is brought out with great incisiveness. In his *Homilies on the Book of Exodus* (VIII) he reminds his hearers that they are the new and true Israel only if they act in such a way that they are worthy of the divine heritage. And he continues: 'If not, if your life is unworthy, then let those people serve as an example to you, who were called to belong to God, but who have deserved to be dispersed among the nations'. Such exhortations are quite frequent in the homilies, though it is not always clear how far Origen applies them to the people as a whole. In the *Homilies on the Song of Songs*, where in view of the concentration of attention on the Church as the pure bride we would least expect it, we find most specific reference to the spiritual dangers by which the Church militant is constantly confronted. Origen does not forget that as yet the Church lives in the old age and says (I, 6) that the blackness of the bride means that she is not yet purified of all taint of sin. Thus we are prepared to hear that there is a time when the bridegroom threatens the bride and says (I, 9): 'Either you will know yourself, for you are a royal bride, wholly beautiful, and I have made you wholly beautiful, for I have made myself a glorious Church without spot or wrinkle, or you must know that, if you do not know yourself and if you ignore your dignity, you will suffer what follows.' It is explained that in that second case the bride will be counted with the goats who are rejected by the good Shepherd. Can it be said more clearly that the new people are not exempt from the judgment of the Lord of the two covenants? And that if it is not what it is meant to be, if it denies its *raison d'être*, it is like salt which has lost its savour and must be thrown away?

★   ★   ★

We come to our third question concerning the Church of the early centuries. It is whether we find in it, as we do in the New Testament Church, the consciousness that the Church needs to be constantly renewed by the Holy Spirit? It is not easy to find evidence for the persistence of this insight. In the third Vision of the *Shepherd of Hermas* the old woman who represents the Church suddenly appears as a young woman and it is explained that this means that the spirit of the Christians is renewed through the good news which they have received and that in the same way those who will repent will be rejuvenated. Should we take this vision to mean that the Church is renewed through repentance? This is one possible explanation, but in view of the ambiguous character of the symbolism of the Shepherd it is hard to arrive at a definite conclusion.

In Irenaeus we find a much clearer affirmation. He says that the message (*praedicatio*) which the Church preaches has been deposited in the Church, just as a precious deposit is deposited in an excellent vessel, and that this message renews its youth and renews (at the same time) the youth of the vessel containing it (III, 24). This is an important statement in that it reflects the tension between the indicative and the imperative of St Paul's teaching concerning renewal and applies this to the Church. The vessel, which is the Church, is precious, it is new; but it needs constant renewal and this renewal comes from the *kerugma*.

Tertullian, the defender of the *regula fidei*, has in his later (Montanist) days affirmed that while the rule of faith is fixed the rest of Christian life, that is its discipline and way of life (*conversatio*) 'is subject to the newness of correction'.[1] And by discipline he does not mean merely church law, but the whole of church life as distinct from doctrine.

But it does not seem that the fathers have often spoken of the renewal of Church life. The reason for their silence in this respect is not difficult to find. In the struggle against heresy the main concern of the spokesmen of the Church had become increasingly to prove that everything in its faith and life could be traced back to the very beginnings. Antiquity therefore became the decisive criterion and newness in relation to the Church appeared as something dangerous. This comes out very clearly in the *Commonitorium* of Vincent of Lerins, written at the time when the theology of St Augustine created a great stir in the Church. We can

---

[1] '*Cetera iam disciplinae et conversationis admittunt novitatem correctionis*' (*De Virg., Vol.* 1). See Flesseman, *Tradition and Scripture in the Early Church*, p. 157.

summarize the main points of Vincent in the following way: The real criterion (or canon) of the faith is: universality, antiquity and consent. As he develops this point, it becomes clear that for him the decisive norm is that of antiquity, that is of agreement with the 'ancestors and fathers'. If some new contagion tries to infect the whole Church, then we must cleave to antiquity which cannot be led astray by any deceit of novelty. Everyone should watch out, that if he expresses something in a new manner, he should not say a new thing. (*Ut cum dicas nove, non dicas nova.*)

Does this mean that there is no progress (*profectus*) in religious matters? Certainly there is. But this progress is growth, not change. Change in the Church leads to disaster. The Church conserves its teaching, never changes anything in it, takes nothing away and adds nothing. When the Church is disturbed by the new ideas of the heretics it writes down old traditions and defines in new formulations the old meaning of the faith.

From the point of view of our subject we must make the following observations about this influential theory which dominated the thought of the Roman Catholic Church until the time when the newer theory of development arose, and which is still advocated by many in our time.

It is striking that in the title of Vincent's tract and throughout its pages the word 'newness' (*novitas*) is always used *in malam partem*. Newness is always 'profane newness', it is innovation, novelty, denial of the old and true. Vincent seems to have forgotten that the main biblical meaning of newness is not the one which the Athenians sought, when they spent their time in nothing except telling or hearing something new. This becomes clear in his attitude to St Augustine, for his polemic against the great African doctor of the Church is based on the fact that St Augustine does not merely repeat the thoughts of the fathers but dares to produce not only old but also new things from the treasure of God's Word.[1] It is rather tragic that the one 'canon' which St Paul proposes in the Epistle to the Galatians, namely the new creation, is now replaced by a 'Vincentian Canon' in which we hear only of antiquity, universality and consent.

Vincent says quite explicitly that 'newness should stop to interfere with antiquity' (Cap. XXXII). The burden of the New Testament message would seem to be the opposite, namely that in the life of the Church the old must constantly be transformed by the new.

Are we engaging with Vincent in a 'dialogue des sourds', a conversation such as is held between deaf people when one speaks about the weather and the other about politics? To a certain extent: yes. For Vincent speaks in the first place about the defence of the catholic faith against heresy. And the New Testament message about newness speaks about the total existence of the Christian community in its relation to the new age. But that does not settle the matter. For Vincent makes it quite clear that the principle of antiquity does not merely affect the doctrine and theology of the Church. And the New Testament does not say that renewal has only to do with life and not with faith.

Vincent is certainly right in insisting on faithful adherence to the apostolic faith and in repeating again and again that the Church is to guard what has been entrusted to it (I Tim. 6.20). He is also right that in order to know what that apostolic faith is, we must listen with attention and respect to the witness of the Church through the ages, through which the *depositum fidei* is transmitted to us. But Vincent has become so obsessed by the fear that the old faith once

[1] See *Commonitorium*, edited by R. S. Moxon, Introduction, p. xxx.

delivered to the saints may be lost or adulterated, that he forgets the total biblical context of the warning to Timothy which is the gospel of the dawn of the new age. He does not see that the *depositum fidei* itself contains the message of renewal, and the call to be renewed every day. And so Vincent's canon is not a true 'canon', not an adequate criterion of church life. It does not take the eschatological status of the Church seriously. It admits only of growth according to the inherent law of the Church. It has no place for the powers of the age to come and for renewal by the Holy Spirit.

Antiquity, universality and consent are not enough. The Church is not only concerned with its own oneness, its universality and catholicity, but also with its holiness. And to be holy means to live in the strength of the new age.

It is only in that context that antiquity can find its rightful place. It means then the 'orientation to the centre', to the apostolic *kerugma*, the source of all truth and life in the Church. That *kerugma* is the true antiquity and at the same time the source of renewal. For the Word of God is not bound and new truth breaks forth from it.

Such truth is not mere novelty, and has nothing to do with what Bossuet called *la démangeaison d'innover sans cesse*, the itching to innovate without ceasing. It is the newness of the new age which we cannot make, but which we can receive. In the light of that truth the Church must continuously correct its whole existence and this includes its faith as well as its life, its message as well as its structure. In this way St Augustine, by rediscovering the neglected elements of the total gospel and particularly by listening anew to the Pauline message, corrected the faith of the Church of his time. If Vincent had had his way, this correction would have been condemned as 'profane novelty'. We can only be grateful that in this case Vincent's principle of antiquity was not applied.

★ ★ ★

The general impression which the story of the battle between the old and the new in the first centuries leaves on us is that the right tension between them was not often maintained and that too many victories were won by the advocates of antiquity as the sole criterion. The emphasis on antiquity as the standard of orthodoxy began to colour the whole life of the Church. The vision of the new people became more and more blurred. But that did not mean that the forces of renewal had ceased to operate. Again and again the message of the new life in Christ and of the new people of God would prove irrepressible and force the Church to listen anew.

4

THE RENEWAL OF THE
CHURCH IN HISTORY

WE have remarkable works concerning the external history of the Church, concerning its expansion and concerning its doctrinal development. But we have practically no studies of Church history written from the point of view of the renewal of the Church. This is most regrettable. For the most important contribution which the study of its own history can and should make to the life of the Church is to teach it how its Lord operates through judgment and renewal. If a Church historian, with a thorough knowledge of the life of the Church through the ages and a keen appreciation of the biblical view of God's dealings with his people, would give us a story of the renewals of the Church, we would come to see far more clearly than we do at present, how the Holy Spirit intervenes in the life of the Church and how Church history with its tragic record of error, betrayal, divisiveness and pride is, in spite of everything, fundamentally different from secular history, because of that inexplicable new element which keeps entering upon the stage at the crucial moments. Such a presentation of Church history would show the extraordinary capacity for renewal which characterizes the Christian Church and which distinguishes it from all other societies. It would demonstrate that there is at the centre of the story of the Church, as there is in the story of Israel, a dynamic which does not fit into the categories of idealistic or materialistic philosophies of history. Though it could of course not *prove* that the Holy Spirit is at work in that history (for the work of the Holy Spirit can only be recognized by faith), it would inevitably raise the challenging questions: What is it that makes for the rebirth of the Church when everything in its own life and in the life of the world seems to point to its approaching death? Why is it that the great attempts to suppress it have so often led to its renewal?

For the great renewals of the Church are from the point of view of secular history quite insoluble puzzles. There is in the literal sense of that word no earthly reason why any neutral and objective observer of the church situation in the beginning of the sixteenth century should have expected to see a powerful emergence of biblical Christianity. The students who were contemporaries of John Wesley at Oxford could not possibly foresee that a great spiritual renewal was to break out in Britain. In our own days the observer of the church situation in Germany in the early thirties could hardly have believed that the weakened churches with their uncertain message would put up a determined spiritual resistance against national socialist paganism. And those of us who followed the tragic story of persecution in the early days of the Soviet government in Russia could not have dreamt that, two decades later, the churches in Russia would again be sufficiently strong to make it necessary for the government to make peace with them.

If we would only watch more carefully the signs of the times, especially of our own times, we would never cease to wonder at this astonishing power of renewal which is given to the Church, whenever and wherever it accepts to be renewed. Calvin's word that the story of the Church is a story of many resurrections,[1] is true and its truth ought to colour and dominate our whole thinking about the present and future of the Church. We need not be nervous, when the Church comes under great outward pressure or even when it is persecuted. As Dr Martin Niemöller once said at one of the most critical moments of the church-struggle in Germany: 'The gospel can stand so much more than any of us think.' The Word of God has a curious 'Jack in the Box' quality. It makes itself more clearly heard whenever the voices of the world try to drown it. Thus the Church learns all through its history that 'though our outer nature is wasting away, our inner nature is being renewed every day' (II Cor. 4.16).

This does not mean that the Church is automatically renewed. The promise that the gates of hell shall not overcome it is not given to every society which calls itself 'Church'. It is only given to the body which Jesus Christ calls '*my* Church'. And the great question which every part of the Church or every church-body must ask itself with fear and trembling is therefore: 'Are we in truth in the Church of Jesus Christ?' If the answer is 'yes'—then there is no need to fear, for then the Lord who has overcome the world will defend his people against all danger.

The real danger for every church is therefore not that it will be persecuted, but that it will take for granted that it is in fact the Church of Jesus Christ and will therefore live in a false security. Here again the history of the Church becomes relevant. Have we considered what it means that in the course of history great Christian Churches have been completely or almost completely wiped out? For there is not only the record of Churches which received new life, there is also the record of Churches which died. Two striking

[1] *Commentary on Micah.*

examples are those of the Church of North Africa and of the Nestorian Church in Central Asia and China.[1]

The Church of Africa, that is of the Carthaginian area, had been the Church of Tertullian, of Cyprian and above all of Augustine. The historian Mommsen has said that it was in this province that Christianity became transformed into a world religion. Harnack adds that since the time of St Paul the strongest impulse for the development of Christianity came from this region. Now that great Church, which had produced so many martyrs for the faith, did not live long beyond the time of Augustine. Soon after the Arab conquest it collapsed altogether.

The Nestorian Church has not made a great contribution to the life of Christendom as a whole. But it had shown extraordinary missionary zeal. As early as the seventh century the Nestorian missionaries reached China and according to the Nestorian monument of 779 'the Christian religion was spread over the ten provinces and there were monasteries in every city'. But[2] a century later this Chinese Christian Church had again disappeared.

By the beginning of the fourteenth century the Nestorian Church as a whole had however no fewer than 200 to 250 metropolitans and bishops all the way from India to Siberia and from Bagdad to Pekin (for China had been re-entered). But a century later, after the great persecution under Tamerlane, this great Church had been reduced to a relatively small number of refugees in Kurdistan.[3]

[1] The case of the Orthodox Church in Anatolia—at one time the area of the seven churches of the Book of Revelation and one of the most important centres of Christian life is different, in that its eclipse took the form of expulsion of the (Greek) Christians after the first world war (1922).

[2] Laurence E. Browne, *The Eclipse of Christianity in Asia*, p. 97.

[3] B. J. Kidd, *The Churches of Eastern Christendom*, p. 422.

How must we explain this complete collapse? The obvious answer is that it was due to persecution. But that answer does not suffice, for in the case of North Africa there was no violent persecution and in any case we have several examples in church history of persecuted churches which survived long and violent persecution.

It would seem that there is a more adequate answer. The historians tell us that the Church of North Africa was largely linked to one particular class, one particular language, one particular culture. It was the Church of the Romans, and did not really become the Church of the indigenous population. The Berbers had only been superficially evangelized and the Phoenicians were as it were 'second class Christians, because they had no Christian literature in their mother tongue, not even the Bible'.[1] Many of the natives had joined the sect of the Donatists which was not merely a schism, but 'part of a revolution'[2] against the ruling and foreign element. Similarly the Nestorian Church in China seems to have remained a foreign church. It is typical that the monks who were compelled to return to lay life were dealt with by the 'Controller of aliens'.[3] And here again we find evidence of a great lack of the sense of real evangelism. Thus there is a record of the baptism of 200,000 Kerait Turks by one priest and one deacon.

Thus it would seem that the alliance of the Church with one particular culture and its lack of evangelistic and pastoral concern for the masses of the population can lead to its annihilation. To put this in other words, it is the

[1] Walter Freytag 'The Lesson of North African Church History' in *Lutheran World*, Winter 1954-5. p. 293; cf. C. P. Groves, *The Planting of Christianity in Africa*, pp. 83 ff.
[2] W. H. C. Frend, *The Donatist Church. A Movement of Protest in North Africa*, 1952, p. 336.
[3] Browne, op. cit., p. 99.

institutional egocentricity of a church, its unwillingness to let itself be used by the Spirit, its wrong concept of what constitutes 'success', in short its rejection of the renewal which is offered to it, which may cause its sickness unto death.

But there remains a mystery.

These explanations can only be very tentative. For we all know of Churches which have failed in similar ways, but which have not been wiped out or even found new life.

In the last analysis we cannot judge these Churches. When we ask: why they died—the Lord answers us 'Do you think that these were worse sinners than all the others because they suffered thus? I tell you, no; but unless you repent you will all likewise perish' (Luke 13.1-5). Thus the important thing to learn in this respect is that where there is no repentance the Lord comes in judgment. The words spoken to the Church in Ephesus (Rev. 2.5): 'I will come to you and remove your lampstand from its place, unless you repent' have found their fulfilment and this should be a warning to every Christian church in the world.

★   ★   ★

But, thank God, the judgment which comes to the unrepentant Church does not always take this definitive form. The judgment unto death indicates that the Church has to do with the holy God. But the holy God is the loving God, who does not desire the death of the sinner and whose judgments are therefore in the first instance judgments unto life. A Church which comes 'under the cross' must therefore in the first place realize that (in the words of the Epistle to the Hebrews) God 'disciplines us for our good, that we may share his holiness' (Heb. 12.10). And this is indeed the characteristic response of genuine Christian faith in time of persecution: to thank the Lord that he does not leave his people alone, that he teaches them again to put all their confidence in him, and that in these ways he renews the life of his Church.

It is one of the most impressive aspects of the life of the Church in history that the churches under pressure or under persecution know so much more about the secret of Christian joy than the churches which live in circumstances of tranquillity. Those of us who have had the privilege to be in close personal touch with persecuted churches have again and again had the experience that when we came to them with the intention to console and encourage we found ourselves consoled and encouraged. The New Testament speaks more than once of 'rejoicing in sufferings'. And at first sight this would seem to indicate the perverted attitude of men who value suffering for its own sake. But as we look more closely we find that in these passages (Rom. 5.3 ff.; James 1.2 f.; I Peter 1.5 ff.) suffering is understood as the merciful act of God by which he tests the faith of his people. And the test or trial is at the same time the great opportunity to come to know in the clearest manner the strength which God gives to the weak. The suffering Church which accepts its sufferings as trials to test its faith is the Church which experiences every day how God renews its life.

The main large-scale attempts to arrive at a renewal of church life have been those of the reform councils of the fifteenth century, of the Reformation and the Counter-reformation of the sixteenth century and the so-called further reformation of the seventeeth and eighteenth centuries. It is useful to look at these attempts from the point of view of the understanding of renewal which we have found in the Bible. In the context of this inquiry we can of course not deal with them as fully as they deserve to be dealt with. And we do not take them in their chronological, but rather their logical order. The reform councils and the

Counter-reformation belong together, and so do the Reformation and the renewal movements of the following centuries.

First the *causa reformationis* at the time of the reform councils. In the light of the fact that in the post-Tridentine Roman Catholic Church the demand for large scale reformation is considered a dangerous heresy, it is impressive to find that in this period the outstanding theologians and even the ecumenical councils themselves speak of 'the general reformation of the Church in its head and members'. For that can only mean that the whole Church needs renewal.

At the Council of Pisa a promising beginning was made. For the cardinals adopted a solemn decree according to which whoever of their number would be elected as pope would continue the council until the universal Church would be sufficiently reformed in its head and in its members.[1] The fourth and fifth sessions of the Council of Constance adopted two decrees in which the word 'reformation' occurs no less than five times.

It is well known that this movement for reform failed, because it led to a struggle for power between the councils and the papacy in which the latter was victorious. But this very fact shows that the conception of reform underlying the movement was lacking in depth. Bossuet describes the eighteen 'articles of reformation' adopted at Constance as principally concerned with holding the Roman Curia to its duties.[2] And even such seemingly radical writings as those of Henry of Langenstein deal only with the structural and moral problems of church life and do not go to the real roots of the situation. The question of the radical renewal of

[1] Bossuet, *Défense de la Déclaration de* 1682 (Abrégé édition de 1814), p. 190.
[1] Op. cit., p. 206.

the Church as a whole is not really raised. It is not seen that renewal does not mean structural re-adaptation, but a returning to the Lord of the Church, a repentant listening to his own Word.

The urge for reform did not cease when the reform councils failed. And it remained alive in the Roman Catholic Church even when it rejected Luther's Reformation. Pope Adrian VI, the pope who, according to his epitaph, considered his calling to the papacy the greatest calamity that had happened to him, and who stated openly that he desired 'to destroy that infallibility which certain doctors attributed to the pope',[1] came nearest to a biblical understanding of church renewal. In his instruction of 1522 to the Nuncio Chierigati he stated openly, that just as our Lord had begun by cleansing the temple, so it was now necessary to cleanse the Church, beginning with the Holy See itself, for 'the malady has crept down from the head to the members'. The whole world thirsted for a real reform. His purpose was to render to the Church again its first beauty.[2] But Adrian added that one could only take one step at a time. He remained too much the prisoner of the system to take any important steps during his short term in office.

In 1546 at the second session of the Council of Trent the Legates admonished the Council in an address drawn up by Cardinal Reginald Pole in these words:[3] 'We see judgment beginning with the house of God. . . . This is what Christ foretold, in saying that his priests are the salt of the earth, but that if the salt lose its savour, it is good for nothing more than to be cast out, and to be trodden underfoot. All

[1] Op. cit., p. 49.
[2] The document is reprinted in Yves Congar, *Divided Christendom*, p. 277.
[3] Ibid., p. 278.

these things we are now suffering.' These are truly biblical words. Did the Council listen? Several decisions of the Council concerning many abuses in the life of the Church show that there was a desire for reform in the Council itself. But here again reform did not become basic renewal. The improvements in the moral life and the organizational structure of the Church which the Council adopted, are not the medicine required for such a sickness as Cardinal Pole had diagnosed. Moreover by declaring that the traditions which had been dictated by the Holy Spirit and conserved in the Catholic Church through continuous succession were to be accepted and venerated 'with the same feeling of piety and reverence' as Holy Scripture the Council said in fact that the Church is judge in its own cause and that its criterion of newness is not the new age, but the inherent law of its own life. Thus the judgment of which the Cardinal had spoken was not really understood as a concrete divine judgment.

Was then the Reformation of the sixteenth century a renewal in the full biblical sense of the term? It started as a movement of repentance, of turning again to the Lord of the Church and of counting on his mercy and forgiveness alone. In his *Great Catechism* Luther stated that the whole life of the Church depends on one thing only, namely on daily forgiveness of sins through the Word and the sacraments.[1]

As he began to proclaim his simple message Luther had no idea of the consequences which this proclamation would have. And he did not need and did not want to know. For that was the concern of God. At the critical moment of the Reichstag in Augsburg he wrote to Melanchthon: 'If Moses had wanted to understand the end (that is to say what God's plan with him was) and how he could escape the army of

[1] *Great Catechism*, Third Article.

Pharaoh, Israel would still be in Egypt today.'[1] Thus Luther did not calculate, but went forward in the simple faith that if the Church trusts wholly in the work of the Holy Spirit, it will receive life and life abundantly. The renewal which Luther sought is therefore not an external reform of the institutional life of the Church. In fact the striking thing about Luther is his indifference concerning outward forms. For the 'Word must do it'. And the Word will create its own forms. So the Church which (against Luther's original desire or expectation and as a consequence of the resistance of the Roman hierarchy against renewal) grew up as a result of the new proclamation, was *in principle* an *open* Church, a Church which was on the move and which was to shape its life according to the Word which God would speak to it in each situation. For, as Luther said in the section of the *Great Catechism* which we have already quoted: 'At present we remain only partially pure and partially saintly, in order that the Holy Spirit may always work upon us through the Word and give us every day forgiveness until (we come to) the life, where there will be no forgiveness but wholly pure and wholly saintly men.' Toward the end of his life Luther warned his successors that the Church can never have peace and must expect to be attacked again and again by the devil. He says: 'You who will come after me, pray and live assiduously with the Word of God, keep the little hurricane-lamp burning, be warned and prepared as men who must expect at any moment that the devil break a window or a door or a roof in order to put out the light'.[2]

And in this respect there is little difference between Calvin

[1] Luther (W.A., 50, 475) quoted by Eberhard Müller, *Luther und die Kirche*, p. 12.

[2] Quoted in Heinrich Fausel, *Luther und Melanchton während des Augsburger Reichstages*, Theologische Aufsätze, München, 1936.

and Luther. It is true that Calvin attached greater importance to the outward form of the Church's life. But he was equally convinced that the renewal of the Church is neither a human act nor an isolated event. It is part of the great drama between God and his people. Again and again the Lord calls his people back to himself. When Calvin dedicated his commentary on Isaiah to King Edward of England he described how the people of Israel, and later on the Church, have again and again fallen away from their Lord. The sin and ingratitude of men have sought to destroy the work of God. 'But, now in our time and contrary to all expectation, the Lord has begun to build up what had been destroyed, in order that the true temple might again be restored, at least in rough outline and that in it there should be worship according to the command of the Gospel. A few small men from among the common people have been elected as architects. A heavy and formidable task, even if Satan did not try to hinder it. . . .' And what of the future? Calvin refers to a cynical remark of Erasmus who in his worldly wisdom had suggested that it would probably all lead to nothing and had asked about one of the Reformers: 'What kind of a fellow does Capito expect his tenth successor to be?' Calvin answers: 'He (Erasmus) was convinced that the struggle of the servants of Christ against the evil of the world is just as hopeless as the attempt to let water flow upward. . . .' But he is wrong because he does not consider 'that in the restoration of the ruined Church we give to the Lord the help which he desires and demands, only in such a way that the Reformation of the Church is his firm work'.[1] Calvin recognizes that the Church in this world stands in constant need of the assistance and intervention of the Holy Spirit.

[1] Calvin's *Lebenswerk in seinen Briefen*, I, 392, ed. Schwarz, Tübingen, 1909.

Now it might have been expected that churches who owe their life to this rediscovery of the dynamic biblical message of judgment and grace, of repentance and renewal, would be churches that (in the words of St Paul) would 'walk', that is to say move forward, in newness of life and that they would overcome the persistent tendency toward a static, self-righteous and egocentric way of life. But that expectation has not been fulfilled. The truth is that very soon after the beginning of the Reformation we find signs in the life of the renewed churches that the old leaven is still or again at work. And there can be no doubt that in the following century the churches of the Reformation were hardly convincing witnesses of the message and life of the new creation within the old creation. Their rationalistic orthodoxy, their lack of evangelistic and missionary zeal, their legalism and their institutional self-assertion were victories of the old upon the new. To be sure they still had the great treasure of the open Bible, and, as the future was to show, that was their one chance for further renewal; but for the moment it seemed that the Word of God did not really operate in shaping and reshaping the life of the Church.

What had happened? Had Erasmus after all been right and had it all been in vain? Why have the Reformation churches 'tended to erect a rigid tradition, stabilizing the forms of the Reformation period, and forgetting that the Holy Ghost moves on, and that the Church can only fulfil its mission on earth, when it allows itself to be broken on the anvil of the Word and reformed again and again'.[1]

One possible answer is of course that the Reformers did not meet with the response which they hoped for. Luther confessed in 1526 in his *Deutsche Messe* that he had hoped to

[1] T. F. Torrance, *Scottish Journal of Theology*, September, 1951, p. 290.

gather those who desired earnestly to live as Christians so that they would pray, study the Bible and receive the sacraments together; in other words he really longed to form living, 'gathered' congregations. Why had he not done so? He answered that he had not yet found the people with whom he could create such congregations.

Another possible answer is that the institutional Church, indissolubly linked to society and the state in one vast *Corpus Christianum*, has been too strong for the Reformers. They could not bring themselves to break completely with the sociological forms in which the Church had lived ever since the days of Constantine. And so the inherent law of the institution acted as a strong brake upon their work of renewal.

Still these answers are insufficient. There is another and more fundamental consideration. It is that the very message to which the Church owes its renewal can be so misunderstood as to become an obstacle to renewal. Or to put it more concretely the very message of repentance can be so misrepresented that it may lead to a very unrepentant attitude. That is what happened to the Reformation message. Its central affirmation concerning the justification by faith contained the insight into (what Niebuhr has called) the 'tragic quality of the spiritual life', which 'was never clearly appreciated until the Reformation'.[1] The Reformers drew the full consequences from the truth that the redeemed are not perfect, that they live by grace alone and that individually as well as in their life together in the Church they need constantly to repent. But before long the churches of the repentance began to *boast* about their repentance. The churches ceased to be in the dynamic situation in which the Holy Spirit opens up the Bible anew, for they were confronted with static theories about the Bible rather than with

[1] *The Nature and Destiny of Man*, II, p. 142.

the Bible itself. Even though the original message was still proclaimed, it was no longer proclaimed as a word of actual judgment and grace, but as an established, systematized orthodoxy. And this meant that grace was no longer the *costly* grace of which the Reformers had spoken. It was grace conceived as an automatic law. As Bonhoeffer put it: 'The justification of the sinner in the world degenerated into the justification of sin and the world. Costly grace was turned into cheap grace without discipleship.'[1]

Thus active, dynamic repentance became arrested repentance and reformation was once again followed by deformation. It seemed really, as if Erasmus had hit the nail on the head and that in many ways 'the tenth successors' of the Reformers were not essentially different in their spiritual attitude from the men against whom the Reformers had fought.

But there were many who could not and would not believe that this was the end of the story of God's dealings with his Church. And so we come to the period in which the battle-cry of the 'further reformation' or 'second reformation' was heard. This new generation of reformers formed a very mixed company. Among them were Anglican and dissenting Puritans held together by their common concern with the 'practice of piety', Dutch Calvinists, strongly influenced by English authors, and at a somewhat later stage German Lutherans in turn influenced by the Dutch. Most of them remained in their churches. Some founded new sects. All believed that there was need for a renewal of the Church.

It is interesting, that the now famous expression *ecclesia reformanda quia reformata* has almost certainly been first formulated in this milieu. In the light of the experiences of the

---

[1] Dietrich Bonhoeffer, *The Cost of Discipleship*, London, 1948, p. 44.

century following the Reformation it is now understood that reformation cannot be a single historical act, but is a permanent task of the Church. As far as can be ascertained it is the Dutch theologian Voetius who combined a very orthodox Calvinism with a tendency toward pietism and a great admiration for Thomas à Kempis, who first coined the phrase. For the phrase appears in the writings of two of his friends and disciples and in one of them his name is specifically mentioned in this connection.[1]

What was meant by this new reformation? It was first of all a protest against the coldly objective and rational orthodoxy of the day. Anna Maria van Schurman, the very learned and gifted lady who was first a friend of Voetius and later joined the sect of Labadie, wrote a poem with the title 'Concerning the sad degeneration of the Christians' from which I translate the following lines:

'They teach that Jesus Christ surely our sins will heal
But not that first our soul the pain of sin must feel . . .
God's Son does not give peace, where peace is made with
  sin
The wounded soul alone will feel his oil poured in.'

So the new reformation was to be a renewal of life, an attempt to practise piety, and there was no intention to reform the faith. Through 'prophesyings', conventicles or *collegia pietatis* and through the new popular devotional literature which crossed all frontiers of nation and confession a new opportunity was given to share in the warmth of

[1] Professor J. Lindeboom has found the phrase in the writings of Jodocus van Lodenstein (in 1674) where it is quoted as a saying of 'a learned man' and in the writings of J. Koelman (in 1678) where it is attributed to Hoornbeek 'following in the footsteps of Voetius'.

a message not merely addressed to the intellect, but to the soul and covering the whole of life, including the conscientious problems of Christian behaviour in the world.

There is no doubt that this second reformation had a great and often beneficial effect on the life of the churches. If this attempt at renewal had not been made the result might well have been an almost total petrification of the churches. But we cannot say that it has resulted in a renewal of the life of the churches as such. Why did it not succeed? There would seem to be two reasons. First of all the new reformers were so preoccupied with 'life' that they did in fact shift the whole emphasis to the new, the reborn man. In reaction against a false objectivism they fell into a false subjectivism. In seeking true renewal of life they were so eager to produce visible results, that they stressed the 'already' at the expense of the 'not yet' and so did not maintain the eschatological tension of the New Testament.

The second reason follows from the first. Although the movement began in the Reformation churches and intended at first to work for the renewal of those churches, the majority began soon to despair of such a renewal of the whole. The resistance of orthodoxy and institutionalism combined seemed to make such renewal a hopeless affair. The individualistic orientation led to a weakening of the sense of responsibility for the total Church. It is typical that it was in this milieu that the biblical concept of 'edification' which means the building up of the life of the Church acquired a different meaning, namely the building up of the inner life of the individual.[1] And so this movement resulted in creating groups of consecrated Christians in the churches or in the

[1] See Martin Schmidt on Spener's *Pia Desideria* in *Theologia Viatorum*, 1951, p. 79.

formation of new movements outside the churches, but not in a renewal of the churches as a whole.

We need not continue the story. For these illustrations suffice to make it abundantly clear that in this task of renewal the Church is its own worst enemy. Like other institutions it seeks the security of the status quo. And almost imperceptibly it slides back from the open, dynamic life into which the Holy Spirit pours his gifts, to the closed, introverted life of self-perpetuation. But we have also seen that this need not be its final fate. For if it allows the Word of God to do its creative work, there is always hope for its renewal.

'The existence of Christianity on this earth is a continuously renewed creation,' said Alexandre Vinet.[1] But if that is so, the churches should realize far more clearly than they do that, if they are not re-created and renewed, they are on the way toward degradation. 'The whole history of the Church', says Jacques Ellul, 'is the history of the reformation of the Church by the Spirit. That work must not cease, for Satan who attacks the Church from within does not stop, and the Spirit of God which gives life to the Church by reforming it, does not stop either. . . . The permanent reformation of the Church is therefore the obedience of the Church to the Spirit; it means accepting that God leads his Church forward and changes it, that the Church does not settle down in a revelation which it treats as if it were its own property, but rather that it is constantly on the lookout to receive the new order which the Spirit brings.'[2] For it is precisely by constantly adapting itself to the plan and word of God that the Church has the true stability and the true continuity. There is a truth for and challenge to all churches in the words which appear in the constitutional

[1] Astié, *Esprit d'Alexandre Vinet*, 1861, I, 385.

[2] *Protestantisme français*, Paris, 1945, pp. 150-1.

documents of the Church of South India: 'The uniting churches acknowledge that the Church must always be ready to correct and reform itself in accordance with the teaching of those (the Holy) Scriptures as the Holy Spirit shall reveal it.'

5

THE WAY OF RENEWAL

WE can group the various attitudes to and conceptions of renewal of the Church under six heads. All of these appear in different churches and in different periods of history.

The first is that the very concept of renewal of the Church must be rejected. Renewal has only to do with individual piety and morality. For the Church as such is a perfect society which in the nature of the case cannot be changed, improved or renewed. The life of the Church must therefore be wholly guided by the criterion of antiquity.

A most interesting example of this obsession by the argument of antiquity is the position of the great Bossuet. The basic argument of his famous *History of the Variations of the Protestant Churches* is that the difference between truth and heresy is the same as that between unchangeableness and novelty. According to him the Church never varies in its teaching. In fact 'the catholic truth, which comes from God, has its perfection from the very beginning'.[1] Antiquity is therefore a conclusive and sufficient criterion.

Now it is a curious and rather tragic fact that Bossuet's own life illustrates so clearly that even his own Roman Catholic Church did not in fact maintain this principle. In the great conflict between the French Church and the

[1] 'a d'abord sa perfection', *Oeuvres complètes*, 1864, Tom., VII, 5 and several times repeated on p. 364.

Papacy Bossuet became the defender of the 'Gallican Declaration' which stated that the Gallican privileges must be respected 'since the greatness of the Holy See requires that the laws and customs established with its consent and that of the Church remain invariable' and that a 'decision (of the Pope) is not unalterable unless the consent of the Church is given'. Bossuet's impressive and voluminous defence of this declaration is wholly based on the principle which he had used against the Protestants and on the basis of this principle his case is unanswerable. But the declaration was indignantly rejected by the Vatican. And Bossuet's defence was not published until long after his death. Thus the great defender of the unchangeable nature of the Church against the Protestants found his own basic apologetic principle rejected by his own Church.

The second attitude is that there is renewal in the life of the Church, but only in the sense of development. The principle of antiquity is not given up, but it is completed and relativized by the notion of growth, of increasing realization of the inherent law of the living body. This is the governing concept of the new Roman Catholic ecclesiology as it arose under the influence of romanticism in the early nineteenth century. J. A. Moehler introduced at that time the conception of doctrinal development. For him and his many followers until our day the key to the understanding of the Church is 'the growth of the life of the Church'. One of his most faithful interpreters summarizes his position in these words: 'If the Church and its doctrine were in every respect immutable they would have no history. There must therefore be changeable (variables) elements together with an absolutely immutable foundation.'[1]

It is not difficult to see that this concept of renewal

[1] Ranft in *L'Église est Une. Hommage à Moehler*, p. 123.

provides new opportunities for Christian apologetics in that the 'biological' categories which are used, seem to be in harmony with the concepts of modern science and culture and that the problem of justifying new doctrinal formulations (which Bossuet could not solve) can thus be restated. But the difficulty is that this conception of the Church isolates the image of the 'Body of Christ' from all other images concerning the Church. A true interpretation of that image must surely take into consideration that the Church is also the people of God and the fold of the Shepherd. And if that wider context is taken seriously, it cannot be maintained that the Church has its law of life within itself, for it is then seen that it receives its life ever anew from the God to whom it belongs, that it must ever be gathered by the Shepherd and that the Body is directed by him who is its Head.

The third position with regard to the changing and unchanging elements in the life of the Church is that of the modernist movements which we find in practically all confessions. Their claim is that the renewal of the Church must take the form of an adaptation to the new cultural developments and that not merely at the level of formulation and structural patterns, but at the level of the content of the faith. The *Protestantenverein* in Germany, founded in 1863 in order to gather together the liberal forces in the German Protestant Churches, declared in the first article of its constitution that it stood for 'a renewal of the Protestant Church in the spirit of evangelical freedom and in harmony with the whole cultural development of our time'. For our generation which has witnessed great conflicts between the Church and the ideologies, it is not difficult to realize that this type of renewal tends to lead to a complete self-annihilation of the Church as it adopts a criterion of renewal which is external and foreign to its own life. But it remains surprising that

Christian theologians could forget the eschatological context of newness in the New Testament to such an extent, that they replaced it by its exact opposite, namely conformity to this world.

In the fourth place we have the position of those who take the eschatological nature of renewal seriously, but whose eschatology is exclusively futurist. In their view real renewal can only take place when the present dispensation is wholly replaced by the new dispensation. In the meantime there is only the newness which we receive in faith but this newness has nothing to do with renewal on the historical plane. This has been the teaching of Protestant orthodoxy in various forms. Its result has generally been that the churches accepted their status as churches composed of justified sinners in such a complacent manner that they became defenceless in their dealing with the world.

The very worldliness of the churches has produced a fifth position according to which renewal means the immediate realization here on earth of the 'church without spot and wrinkle'. The firs of the long series of sects which have taken this position, the Montanist movement which described itself as 'the new prophecy', had already all the main characteristics which appear again and again in the sects of later periods of history. It reacted against the increasing worldliness of the official Church, it sought to create a fellowship of awakened Christians,[1] it believed in special revelation over and above the biblical revelation, it proclaimed a *novissima lex* to be followed. And it did all this on the basis of an apocalyptic type of eschatology. It is at this last point that its weakness can best be shown. For in this respect it breaks the balance between the 'not yet' and the 'already'

---

[1] According to Epiphanius, Montanus said, 'Men sleep, I awaken them'.

which we found to be the New Testament perspective. It is not the task of the Church to act as if the new age had wholly replaced the old age. The 'angelic fallacy' of the apocalyptic sect is a challenge in that it reminds the Church of the constant danger of worldliness, but, in spite of its impressive insistence on genuine renewal of life, it must not tempt us to think that renewal once for all, perfected renewal such as will characterize the 'church without spot or wrinkle', can be attained in this world.

The sixth position is that which we try to develop in these lectures.

★   ★   ★

Luther once described the pilgrimage of the Church in the following concentrated formula: 'It is not yet done and accomplished, but it is going on. It is not the end, but the way. It is not all glistening and shining, but it is all being swept.'[1] We must now try to describe that way of renewal and that process of cleansing.

The starting point is that the renewal of the Church is the work of God and not of man by himself. That is not meant as a pious reminder that we need the help of God in all that we undertake. It is meant in a much more radical sense. All that we have found in the Old and New Testament confirms that the renewal of the Church means first of all the creative work of God among his people, the victories won by the new age over the old age. The Church does not renew itself: it is the object of God's work of renewal. 'Be ye renewed' does not mean: 'Get busy and find some different and better method of Christian action.' It means: 'Expose yourself to the life-giving work of God. Pray that he may make the dry bones come to life. Expect great things

[1] Martin Luther, *Ausgewählte Werke. Calwer Ausgabe*, 5, 154.

from him. And get ready to do what he commands.'

This is a very practical truth. For it implies that the renewal of the Church does not begin with more or less solemn decisions of synods, conferences or committees, but with an encounter between God and men, in which God takes hold of the situation and empowers them to serve as his instruments of renewal.

Must we then always wait for God before taking any action for the renewal of the Church? Yes, but our waiting must be waiting in the biblical sense. 'As the eyes of servants look unto the hand of their masters and as the eyes of a maiden unto the hands of her mistress, *so* our eyes wait upon the Lord our God' (Ps. 123.2). We know that he is the living God, who makes all things new. We know that he desires his Church to be the centre of new life in an old and passing world. So we must be continually on the watch for the initiatives which he will take. It is inevitable that the Church living within a world which knows no real renewal, falls again and again into the worldly way of just 'going through the motions' of church life and thus becomes part of the world. But it is equally inevitable that the Lord who has created the Church and given it newness of life rescues it continually from its worldliness. The Church must be renewed, because it has been renewed. We have therefore sure ground for our hope that God will not leave the Church alone in our day and generation. And we have good reason to expect him to give us clear guidance as to the specific task which he desires us to accomplish for the renewal of the Church today.

But how and where do we discover what renewal according to God's will means? Every true renewal of the Church is based on the hearing anew of the Word of God as it comes to us in the Bible. This seems at first sight impossible. How can the new result from a return to the old? There have therefore been many who have sought the renewal of the Church by breaking away from the Bible or by adding to and improving upon the Bible. But we must maintain this simple truth that outside the Word of God there is in this world no true source of renewal. Why is that so? Because the Bible is the authentic record of the only radically new event that has ever taken place in the world. All other newness is either borrowed from that event or it is only newness in appearance. If the Church which seeks to renew itself takes its lead from some new religious or cultural development or some new technique, it remains in fact within the closed circle of the old world. If it turns for inspiration to some period of its own past it is not directly in touch with the source. It can only break out of the old world and enter into living touch with the new world by submitting itself to the judgment and inspiration of God's revelation itself and that revelation is given to us through the Holy Scriptures. Here alone a true dialogue can take place between the Church and its Lord. Here the Church discovers that it needs renewal and what renewal means. This 'orientation to the centre' (Cullmann) has been and is the great life-giving force in the Church and this is the true return to the source. In saying this we do not forget the work of the Holy Spirit. As we have seen, the New Testament teaches with the greatest clarity that there is no renewal except through the Holy Spirit. The Bible is a dead letter if the Spirit does not make it the living Word of God for us. But it is wholly unbiblical to oppose the spirit and the Word of God or to separate them from each other. The Spirit does not speak 'on its own authority' but speaks 'whatever he hears'. He 'takes what is mine', says Jesus (John 16.13-14). And all appeals to the Spirit which seek to by-pass the historical record of the actual work of the Lord are therefore appeals to the spirit of man rather than to the Holy Spirit.

Karl Barth says: 'Since the Church has been called into being by the Word of the new birth and the new creation, it cannot maintain its life except through this Word. What is the use of all natural vitality even if it is so great that it enables the Church to win the whole world? In that way the Church can maintain some kind of life as one of the institutions which are hastening to their death. But as the Church of truth and of eternal life it is dead, right in the midst of the most flourishing development, if the word of truth withdraws itself from it.'[1] And we can also put this the other way round. A church which has nothing but the living Word, a church which is attacked on all sides but has this one defender, is a church which need not fear for its life, for its youth is renewed like the eagle's (Ps. 103.5). It is in listening to the Word of God in the Scriptures that the Church discovers again and again what God's design is and what its own place is in that design. Where else can it find out about the total plan of God and come to know what particular mission he has assigned to the Church? Where else can it come to realize the full content of its own life and come to understand its own past and its own future?

It is through the Bible and the Bible alone that the Church can and must recover the eschatological dimension of its own existence. A Church in which the Bible has the last word is bound to be forcefully reminded of its very *raison d'être* as a first fruit of the new age and will therefore be saved from conforming itself to the world. And a Church in which the Bible has the last word will never be able to forget that it is not the Kingdom of God, and that it lives under the constant judgment of the Kingdom of God. Thus

[1] *Kirchliche Dogmatik*, I, 2,772.

it will be saved from the solitude and self-centredness of a sterile monologue. And thus it will be driven to constant self-criticism.

The tragedy of a Church which does not give to the Bible the decisive place in its life is that it loses the eschatological perspective, that it becomes increasingly tempted to consider its own existence as an aim in itself and that it thus loses the capacity for radical self-criticism and renewal of life. This is illustrated in the story of the medieval Church and especially in the use it made of St Augustine's conception of the Church. In *De Civitate Dei* St Augustine had made the crucial affirmation: 'So the Church now on earth is both the Kingdom of Christ and the Kingdom of Heaven'.[1]

Now St Augustine was far too profound a theologian to maintain that identification without qualification. And so we find in his writings strong tension between the conception of the Church as the Kingdom (or at least as part of it)[2] and the eschatological affirmation that the Church in this world is still a Church of strangers and pilgrims. Thus he affirms: 'The whole Church says: Forgive us our sins. She has therefore spots and wrinkles. But in the confession of sins the spots are washed away, the wrinkles taken away'.[3] Now the medieval Church did not follow St Augustine in his eschatological emphasis, but embraced his teaching concerning the identity of the Church and the Kingdom. And on the basis of this so-called 'Augustinianism' the Church became that proud institution living its own autonomous life which found its full expression in the medieval papacy.

Now it is a curious fact that even in the Reformation this

[1] *De Civitate Dei*, Book XX, ch. 9.

[2] *De Civitate Dei*, Book XIX, ch. 17; cf. Harnack, *Dogmengeschichte*, III, p. 136.

[3] *Serm.* 181.7. Quoted by Grosche, *Pilgernde Kirche*, p. 67.

erroneous identification of the Church with the Kingdom of God was at first maintained. Martin Bucer says quite definitely that the Kingdom of God is the Church of Christ.[1] Beza did not speak otherwise. So whatever we may think of his real motives, Thomas Hobbes had a real point when in his *Leviathan* he accused both the Roman Catholics and the Protestants of identifying the Church and the Kingdom and of thus confusing promise and fulfilment.[2]

What William Temple has said of the Roman Catholic Church is to a certain extent true of other Churches too. He says: 'All the doctrinal errors of Rome come from the direct identification of the Church as an organized institution, taking its part in the process of history, with the Kingdom of God.'[3] The Church needs to remember all the time that, in the excellent phrase of an Anglo-Catholic theologian, it 'is the body, alike of sin and of glory, 'at once the object and the instrument of the judgment and salvation of God'.[4]

★　　　★　　　★

There can therefore be no renewal without repentance.

All great renewals in the history of the Church have been movements of *repentance*. This is inevitable because renewal presupposes a break with the old world. We have noticed that the restoration of the Covenant in Israel was conditional upon true repentance. In the New Testament repentance is the burden of the message of Jesus; it is the climax of St Peter's preaching at Pentecost; it is the key-word of the

---

[1] Courvoisier, *La Notion de l'Église chez Bucer*, p. 70.

[2] *Leviathan* (1651), pp. 334, 341, 385.

[3] Iremonger, *William Temple*, p. 420; cf. the Encyclical *Quas Primas* of 1925: 'The Church is precisely this Kingdom of Christ destined to cover the whole world.'

[4] Dom Gregory Dix, quoted in *Catholicism To-day* (The Times), p. 39.

letters to the seven churches of Asia in the Book of Revelation. Thus Martin Luther went straight to the centre, when
in the first of his theses which he nailed to the church door
in Wittenberg in 1517 he said: 'When our Lord and Master
Jesus Christ says Repent, he means that the whole life of the
faithful is to be a life of repentance.'

What does this mean? For Luther repentance is the
dynamic element in the Christian life. Where there is no
repentance, there can only be the static, old existence which
is tantamount to death. In his Commentary on Romans of
1515-16 (on Rom. 12.2) he explains that life is not to stand
still but to move on. The Christian moves from sickness to
health. His life is a passage from sin (which is non-being)
through repentance (which is becoming) to righteousness
(which is being). The Christian is always *in fieri*, in process
of becoming, and repentance or the new birth is the transi-
tion from sin to righteousness. This conception corresponds
to the dialectic between the old and the new man in the
epistles of St Paul. And it is just as true of the Church as it is
of the individual Christian.

We must then not think of repentance as a quietistic and
introverted preoccupation with the sins of the Church. On
the contrary we must think of it as the opening of the doors
of the cage in which the squirrel can only go through the
vain repetition of the same monotonous movements. Repentance is turning from the old world to the new, from the
past to the future, from the closed world to the open heaven,
from egocentricity and church-centredness to God's Kingdom. Since repentance implies a rupture with the old, it
means the concrete liberation of the Church from the various
forms of enslavement and imprisonment to which it has submitted itself. We shall have to come back to this point when
we discuss the renewal of the Church in its relation to the

world. But we must say in this connection that the recovery of the total independence of the Church is an essential condition of all renewal. For the chief characteristic of the old, unrenewed condition of the Church is precisely its dependence upon and imitation of the ways of the present age. All through the history of Israel the great temptation is to follow the example of the other peoples, to cease being 'different'. And for the New Testament the temptation is to be conformed to this world which (according to Rom. 12.2) is the exact opposite of renewal in Christ. For this world is, as Calvin puts it: the *scopus veteris hominis*, that is the field of activity of the old man.

The liberation of the Church does not mean that it turns its back upon the world, but that it becomes again wholly dependent upon its Lord, does not listen to the voice of strangers and is in the midst of this world the spokesman of the Word of God which is not fettered (II Tim. 2.9). Thus every renewal of the Church is in one sense a movement of withdrawal from the world and from entangling alliances in the political, social, cultural or philosophical realms. But that withdrawal is never an aim itself. It is a withdrawal with the purpose of returning to the attack.

★　　★　　★

Church-renewal also means *re-edification* of the Church. In the New Testament edification is not used in the subjective sense of intensification and nurture of personal piety. It means the action of the Holy Spirit by which he creates the people of God and gives shape to its life. In Ephesians ch. 4 *oikodome* is the upbuilding of the Body of Christ. In I Peter, ch. 2 *oikodomein* is the building of the spiritual house or house of the Spirit. And this reference to the Church as the work of God is included whenever the expression 'edification' is used. 'The object of edification is not in the first place the individual, but the whole, the Church', says Karl Ludwig Schmidt.[1]

In one sense the Church *has* been built; but in another sense it is constantly being built and rebuilt.[2] The task of men is to 'let themselves be built up', but it is also to participate in the work of the Holy Spirit and to build up or edify each other.

What does this mean concretely? It means to make the Church what it is in essence, to realize its destiny, to make it manifest in the world as the holy nation, as God's own people (I Peter 2.9). Karl Ludwig Schmidt has called attention to the relationship between *oikos* (house) and *oikodomein* on the one hand and *paroikia* on the other.[3] Now this word *paroikia*, from which our word 'parish' (*paroisse*) is derived, really refers to the fact that Christians live in this world as people who have no abiding city in this world (Heb. 13.14), but who have their commonwealth (or citizenship) in heaven (Phil. 3.20). They live in this world as strangers and pilgrims (I Peter 2.11). To build the Church is therefore not to build up a solid institution which is wholly at home in the world and uses the methods of the world. It is rather to organize a band of pilgrims who are on the way to a new and better country and who must therefore not adapt themselves to their temporary surroundings.

It would seem that this New Testament conception of churches which are by their very nature churches in exile cannot possibly have any relevance for our congregations

[1] K. L. Schmidt in *Wesen und Aufgabe der Kirche in der Welt*, 1946, p. 20.

[2] 'Die immer neu zu vollziehende, sich vollziehende Konstitution, die *creatio continua* der Kirche' (Vielhauer cited by Bornkamm, *Das Ende des Gesetzes*, p. 117).

[3] K. L. Schmidt, loc. cit., p. 26.

which have become so firmly rooted in the world and which often pride themselves on the fact that, so far from being exiles, they are the most stable element of the society in which they live. But that only shows how badly we need to hear the New Testament message of renewal with its all-pervading eschatological perspective. And is it not true that the degeneration of much of our church life comes precisely from the fact that it has lost its 'otherness' in relation to the world and that men no longer see any noticeable difference between the Church and any other society which is concerned with spiritual or moral uplift? Our congregations can only be built up and renewed, if we recover the sense of the unique place of the Church in God's plan and history and show the world that it is precisely because of this uniqueness that the Church has a word of hope for the life of the world.

*　　　*　　　*

The building up of the Church means at the same time the restoration of true *fellowship* in our congregations. For the New Testament *koinonia* belongs to the very nature of the Church. And what does this mean? It means partnership in a common calling, sharing in the same spiritual gifts and above all common participation in the Body of Christ. This is most simply expressed in the formula the '*koinonia* (fellowship) of the Holy Spirit', for that means, really, participation in the Holy Spirit. This fellowship cannot be created, where there is nothing to participate in except human sentiments. And the renewal of this fellowship depends on the re-entry of the Church into the realm of the new creation. Where that happens a congregation ceases to be an amorphous mass of people, becomes a true family of God and fulfils its function of showing the world how God desires men to live together.

In one sense the Church is definitely an otherworldly Church, for it knows that it belongs to the new world, which is indeed another world in relation to the old world. But that 'otherworldliness' has nothing to do with an egotistic enjoyment of the blessings of individual salvation or with indifference concerning the life of the present world. For the *raison d'être* of the Church is to announce the good news of the new creation in Christ. It is not a refuge for saved souls; it is a band of messengers or, to use a very typically biblical word, of 'heralds' who proclaim the good news of the Kingdom and of the entrance of that Kingdom in this world in the person of Jesus Christ. These heralds are not self-appointed; they are commissioned by Christ. They do not invent a message of their own. They speak of what they have seen and heard (Acts 4.20).

★   ★   ★

The renewal of the Church implies therefore also that the Church rediscovers its *apostolic*, missionary character. This will express itself first of all in that its witness to its own members becomes again a true *kerugma*, that is to say the proclamation of the great deeds of God and the events through which he has intervened in the world for the salvation of men. And thus the witness itself will become an event. For true preaching is not talking about God and even less talking about our own experiences and ideals. It is (to use a magnificent phrase of Bernard Lord Manning) 'a manifestation of the Incarnate Word, from the written word, by the spoken word'.[1] As P. T. Forsyth put it—many years before Karl Barth began to hammer on this truth—'God's living word reproduces itself as a living act'. And the question is: 'Does the Gospel

[1] Bernard Lord Manning, *A Layman in the Ministry*, p. 138.

preach itself through us with power? Are our sermons deeds, action-sermons?'[1]

But renewal means at the same time that the evangelistic and missionary task is seen as the normal task of the whole Church. Evangelism and missions, not as a peculiar and somewhat peripheral concern of a special group of church members, not as one of many activities to which one contributes one's gifts of money, but as the inevitable expression of the understanding which the Church has of its own nature and calling. This can only come through the work of the Holy Spirit. But the gift is precisely promised to the Church for this purpose. 'You shall receive power when the Holy Spirit has come upon you and you shall be my witnesses in Jerusalem and in all Judea and Samaria and to the end of the earth' (Acts 1.8).

★ ★ ★

We have seen that the renewal of the Church is in a very literal sense a superhuman task. The old world seems always to have the advantage of the conflict. Every intervention of the Holy Spirit appears as a partial intervention and all true newness in the Church seems to lead a precarious existence. Every time the work of renewal has to be begun all over again. There is in the life of the Church in history no definitive renewal, no renewal which is not threatened by relapse into old ways, no reformation which is not followed by some form of deformation. But if we conclude that therefore the situation of the Church is hopeless we are wholly at variance with the biblical view.

According to the Old and New Testament, the people of God live in the dangerous, insecure situation that nothing in

[1] P. T. Forsyth, *Positive Preaching and the Modern Mind*, 1949 (first edition in 1907), pp. 55 and 57.

their own life is ever a definitive, finished achievement. The Church is not itself the new creation; and it needs constantly to be renewed by judgment and repentance. But this is not a reason for despair. For the miracle is the miracle of God's grace, of his patience and forgiveness. The miracle is the faithfulness of God who does not leave his people alone, but continues to work at their salvation. The miracle for which we can never be grateful enough, is that the Holy Spirit continues to plead with the Church 'Be transformed by the renewal of your mind' and that through him the Church is actually renewed.

6

THE NEW CHURCH IN THE
OLD WORLD

WHAT are the implications of the renewal of the Church for its attitude in and to the world? We have already seen that the Church is to witness in word and deed to the new creation within the life of the old creation. But this formula which seems so self-evident in the light of the New Testament sounds totally unrealistic if we apply it to the empirical life of the Churches as they are. The Church as the representative of radical renewal in an old world? Millions of men today would consider this claim as a good joke, for to them the Church is exactly the opposite: namely the guardian and spokesman of all that is decrepit and antiquated in a world which is being radically transformed by new ideologies and new techniques.

Our answer to these critics cannot and must not be to deny that there is a gulf between the fundamental claim which the Church makes and the reality of its life. On the contrary! If we are to speak convincingly to the world, we shall have to make it abundantly clear that we are fully aware of the existence of that gulf. We shall have to show that we know better than any outsiders in which ways the churches deny their very *raison d'être*. And we shall have to make clear why we believe in spite of that obvious contradiction between its message and its life, that the Church is and remains the bearer of the eternal promises of God.

The basic reason why we believe this is that God continues to work upon his people, that Jesus Christ is the living Christ who remains with his Church and that the Holy Spirit is ever active.

This treasure of the faithfulness of God, of the presence of Christ, of the activity of the Holy Spirit, is not given in such a way that the churches themselves become pure images of the life and work of the triune God. The treasure is offered to us in and through earthen vessels. St Paul makes perfectly clear why this must be so. It is in order 'to show that the transcendent power belongs to God' (II Cor. 4.7). Thus the Church is reminded that it is only a tool in the hands of God. But this is in no sense a reason for the Church to 'take it easy'. In every time and in every situation it must ask itself whether its admittedly earthly existence really serves to manifest the transcendent, creative, purifying and renewing power of God.

In order to show what this means in practice we will deal with three aspects of the life of the Church in the world.

Our first point is this: *It is a fact that the churches allow themselves to be imprisoned by the world, but it is also true that imprisoned churches can be and are liberated by the Holy Spirit.*

In what sense do the churches become imprisoned churches? In the sense that they enter consciously or unconsciously in alliance with secular forces and that these alliances become entangling alliances which restrict or jeopardize the freedom of the churches. This subject of the impact of secular life upon the churches is not a popular subject in ecclesiastical or theological circles. Very little thorough study has been made of it. The remarkable volumes of Max Weber, Ernst Troeltsch and R. H. Tawney, which made us aware of the somewhat discreditable relationships between spiritual events and economic and social developments, have not been taken as seriously as they deserve to be taken. And the Marxist challenge according to which all religious developments are to be explained in terms of economic factors has not been adequately answered. We go on talking and acting as if the life of the churches is wholly and exclusively dominated by theological and spiritual factors. But this blindness to the mundane realities makes us defenceless and impotent in resisting the invasion of secular forces into the Church.

The fact is that the life of every church is to a large extent shaped by social, economic, political, cultural, national and racial factors which reflect the secular environment in which this particular church has grown up. These factors are not necessarily dangerous for its integrity as a Christian church. Thus the use of a national language is first of all a means of effective evangelism. And there is nothing inherently wrong in the use of thought forms which belong to the culture of a specific country or period. But everyone of these factors can become a link in the chain which binds the church to the world. And the most insidious forces are those which are hardest to recognize because they seem self-evident and can only be unmasked by the critical outsider or by the insider with unusual spiritual sensitivity.

Take for instance the bourgeois or middle-class character of the great majority of the churches today. The sarcastic intellectual and the Marxist with his class-consciousness are immediately struck by the fact that in such external things as manners and dress but also in weightier matters such as social and individual ethics the life of the Church reflects so very largely the mentality of the in-between class. One of the most serious obstacles to evangelism in our time is that it is so difficult to make an intellectual or a worker who has discovered the truth of the gospel feel at home in our congregations. But since most members of the Church are themselves products of bourgeois mentality, only deep spiritual insight will make them aware of the syncretism, the mixture of Christianity and class atmosphere which has come to dominate their church life.

And the same is true with regard to national and cultural influences. Unwittingly we allow the Church to be entangled by alliances with national sentiment, national policies, national forms of organization. It seems so obvious that churches should associate themselves with national concerns that we forget to ask just at which point the Church ceases to witness to the Lordship of Christ over the nations. Arnold Toynbee in his *Study of History* has a chapter on the pernicious influence of the doctrine that the secular authorities should have a determining influence on religion and comes to the devastating conclusion that 'the effect of the unholy *mariage de convenance* between religion and politics was to make religion itself anathema'. He considers that the modern indifference to religion is largely the outcome of the alliance between the Church and the *raison d'état* and draws this conclusion: 'We are still reacting against a subordination of religion to politics which was the crime of our sixteenth century and seventeenth century forbears.'[1] Now that warning should not only be taken to heart by churches which have official relationships with the state but also by churches which, though theoretically quite independent, tend to identify themselves with specific national groups or political attitudes. In the modern world with its fierce ideological strife, statesmen and politicians seek constantly to use the Church for ends which are essentially different from the one

[1] *A Study of History*, Vol. V, pp. 670-1.

and only purpose for which the Church exists. Many churches are imprisoned in ideological fronts and exploited for secular goals without realizing what they are doing.

But there is, thank God, another side to this story. Whatever the Marxists may say, the Church is not merely a product of its sociological environment. The Church which has been invaded by foreign forces can be liberated. When the Church realizes again that it is the creation of the Holy Spirit, that it lives 'by every word that proceeds from the mouth of God' (Matt. 4.4) and that 'the Word of God is not fettered' (II Tim. 2.9) the great process of liberation sets in and the Church which had seemed to become a mere reflection of society or, as Karl Marx called it, nothing but the 'spiritual aroma of the world',[1] emerges in its true and original character as the witness of the new creation which, instead of conforming itself to the world, demands the transformation of the world. It is the privilege, but also the solemn obligation of the churches which confess that the Church can and must live by the strength of the Word of God alone, to show again and again that that Word is a liberating word. It is impressive to find that this is also understood by some Roman Catholic theologians. Writing in *Irénikon*, the well-known periodical of the Benedictine Priory of Amay in Belgium, Father D. N. Oehmen states: 'The historical vocation (of Protestantism) seems to be to react with the extreme intransigence of the prophet against the secularization of the Church which is always threatening and always active.' And he adds that in the economy of salvation Protestantism has its *raison d'être* not only in relation to the western Church, but to the whole Church.[2]

We live in a time in which this process of renewal through

---

[1] *Oeuvres philosophiques*, Tome I, 84.
[2] *Irénikon*, Vol. XXI (1948), p. 26.

liberation finds clear expression. The paradox of the situation is that in many cases secular forces which seek to weaken the Church by withdrawing any form of support from it are in fact contributing to its renewal. Thus the younger churches in Asia which were in danger of being too closely linked with western culture or even western political influences, find a new independence and vigour now that they live under non-Christian governments. But it may well be that the most impressive example of such an involuntary contribution to the renewal of the Church will be furnished by communism. It happens that many of the churches in countries which have today communist régimes, were so closely bound to the state or to a more or less feudal social system, that they were largely immobilized. Now the communist system, while keeping a close watch over the churches forces them to live wholly and exclusively on the spiritual resources which are given to the Church. They can no longer count on the help of national tradition or of political power. So it becomes a question of life and death whether they find true renewal through the preaching of the gospel. In other words where the churches in these countries are aware of their *kairos*, Marxism is in fact working for the renewal of the Church. We may some day be able to say that just as King Cyrus was used by the Lord to liberate the Jews from captivity, so communism has been used to give to several churches a new sense of fundamental independence from men and a new understanding of their unique mission.

Our second main point about the renewal of the Church in its relation to the world is this: *It is true that the churches tend to be self-centred, but it is also true that through the power of the Holy Spirit self-centred churches can be and are transformed into bearers of the good news to all men.*

Churches cannot only be imprisoned by the world; they

can inflict imprisonment upon themselves and become the victims of an institutionalism which has no other aim than self-perpetuation and self-assertion. No one who has come to know the life of many churches can deny that this danger of institutional self-centredness exists in all of them and that in many cases it acts as an almost insuperable obstacle to all renewal.

Among the causes of the breakdowns of civilization Arnold Toynbee emphasizes especially 'the intractability of institutions'[1] and shows that the force of inertia which is inherent in all institutions tends to work against renewal. Now this danger arises in a special way in ecclesiastical institutions, because they are not only hallowed by antiquity, but also and especially by their real or supposed association with doctrinal convictions. There is a *real* association between the institutional and the doctrinal in so far as the structure of the Church is based on a conception of the nature of the Church as it is revealed in the New Testament. But since the Church lives in the world and in history it is inevitable that many secular factors enter into its organizational life. And the tragedy is that these secular factors are not recognized for what they are, but are considered as no less holy and intangible than the doctrinal foundation. Thus the affirmation that the Church is holy can easily be taken to mean that the forms in which the Church has traditionally expressed itself are holy. And once that step has been taken, real renewal becomes a practical impossibility.

It is true that all churches admit in principle that there are aspects of their life for which they cannot claim permanent validity and which are therefore subject to renewal or reformation. Even the Roman Catholic Church, the most institutionalized of all Churches, can therefore speak of reformation. The very comprehensive analysis which

[1] *A Study of History*, IV, 133 ff.

Father Congar has made of true and false reform in the Church[1] shows that it is possible to take one's stand on the tenets of Roman Catholic theology and at the same time to advocate renewal in many aspects of church life. Thus Father Congar can say that the Church is in a process of continuous self-reformation and lives only by reforming itself.[2] And it is of course a fact that in our own time we see remarkable movements of spiritual renewal operating in Roman Catholicism. On the other hand this same study shows very clearly that the limits within which such movements must remain are very narrow. They may occupy themselves with the *état de choses*, that is to say the area of human custom and accidental historical form. But they must not go any further and dare not raise questions about any of the many matters upon which the Church has taken a stand. The fact that the *ex cathedra* decisions of the Pope are irreformable means that the whole life of the Church is dominated by a principle of irreformability and that forces of renewal, while they may go far in many and important directions, can never touch the life of the Church as a whole.[3]

We might expect that churches which do not attach this weight to tradition and distinguish sharply between the Church and the Kingdom of God are not inclined to the error of treating their institutional forms as sacrosanct. But this is not the case. Father Congar rightly calls attention to the extraordinary role which traditions play in fact in the life of churches which deny in theory that tradition has any

[1] *Vraie et fausse Réforme dans l'Église*, Éditions du Cerf.

[2] Op. cit., p. 21.

[3] Thus the Encyclical *Pascendi dominici gregis*, quoting Leo XIII, even disapproves of references to 'a new order of Christian life, new teachings of the Church, new needs of Christian souls, a new social calling of the clergy, a new Christian humanism' and states that the bishops must not allow such expressions in books or in teaching.

authority of its own. It is true that many Reformation churches defend their specific systems of organization or their ecclesiastical customs with a zeal which ought to be reserved for the defence of the faith itself. The great tragedy is that such institutionalism breeds a type of mentality which puts survival of the institution above every other consideration. The ecclesiastical machinery must be kept going. Unconsciously opportunism and diplomacy take the place of thinking and acting in the simple confidence that the Lord of the Church guides his people. Thus institutionalism becomes a main obstacle to renewal, for (to put it in the words of Toynbee) 'all energies are absorbed in the effort of maintaining the position which they have attained already, and there is no margin of energy left over for reconnoitring the course of the road ahead, or the face of the cliff above them, with a view to further advance'.[1]

But here also we need not become obsessed with the human, all too human, side of the story. The Holy Spirit works mightily to save the churches from this self-inflicted imprisonment and breaks through the hardened institutionalized forms. For the Church is not meant to live unto itself but for that ministry of reconciliation through which God reconciles the world to himself. It is to be apostolic. And apostolic means above all to act as an apostle, as one who is sent out into the world to render witness to Christ.

The most impressive example of the way in which the Holy Spirit deals with an introverted Church is to be found in the New Testament itself. The Book of Acts shows us that at the outset the apostles did not live up to their apostolic mission. They did not go out to the ends of the earth and did not witness to the Gentiles until they were forced to do so by the great outsider, who was not a 'normal' apostle—

[1] *A Study of History*, IV, 30.

St Paul. And is not his fight for the true apostolicity of the Church also a fight against an incipient clericalism in which the Church takes its own institutional aspect too seriously? That would seem to be implied in the story of Galatians 2 where St Paul speaks of the authorities in Jerusalem as 'those who were reputed to be something' and adds: 'what they were makes no difference to me.'

In the course of church history the figure of the 'outsider' entrusted with the mission to call the Church away from its preoccupation with its own existence and to face it with the challenge of its evangelistic task in and to the world, is found again and again. In fact the whole modern missionary movement began as a movement of outsiders who had to break through the hardened walls of institutional inertia in their churches. And the story of the Christian youth movements and of many vital lay movements in the nineteenth and twentieth centuries is similar. The grave questions which arise in all these cases are whether on the one hand the outsiders 'go to Jerusalem' as St Paul did, that is to say whether they really seek the renewal of the Church in its wholeness and on the other hand whether the 'authorities' offer to the 'outsiders' the right hand of fellowship so that they can fulfil their function within the Church rather than outside it. Where these two questions are answered affirmatively these movements have become a powerful force of renewal in the churches.

The area in which this whole question is most acute today is surely that of evangelism. For the situation in most churches is that while there is a desire to evangelize, very little effective evangelism takes place. The Church does not find the way to those large masses of the people who have become religiously indifferent. And one of the main reasons for this inability to reach the unchurched is precisely the lack of adaptability of the Church to the demands of the new situation. But, thank God, there are men and women in many churches who see that the old forms of church life do not suffice and who show spiritual imagination in their approach to the masses. The *Kirchentag* in Germany with its simple direct appeal to the layman; the industrial chaplaincies which carry the witness right into the life of the factory; the lay groups which seek to proclaim Christian truth in terms of their daily secular vocation are some of the signs that the apostolic task of the Church is being rediscovered.

But the big question is as yet unsolved, namely whether the time has not come for far more radical changes in the life of the Church, in order to make it an effective instrument for the accomplishment of its apostolic task in the world today. Dare we maintain unchanged ecclesiastical institutions which are so largely set up for the purpose of merely keeping the Christian flock together? Should we not adapt our life to the new task of evangelizing the millions outside the churches? Already in some countries the old ecclesiastical bodies have largely been destroyed and the effect has not been a weakening of the Church, but rather a strengthening of its evangelistic effectiveness. Some time the challenge comes to each church whether it is willing to sacrifice its institutional life in order to gain the apostolic life.

Our third point concerning the attitude of the Church to the world is this: *It is true that the message of the Church to society often lacks the qualities of true spiritual authority and concreteness and thus becomes irrelevant, but it happens again and again that the Holy Spirit uses the churches to speak the most needed, that is the prophetic word to the world.* It is no longer necessary to argue that it is an essential part of the Church's task to speak to the world. Practically all churches have rediscovered this. But the question remains just what the nature of that prophetic voice is. And that question is all the more important since there is an alarming disproportion between the quantity of resolutions, messages and reports which the Churches issue in this connection and the (positive or negative) effect which these statements produce. Now it would be all too easy to conclude that this lack of reaction is wholly due to the indifference of the world. For it is quite clear that a great deal of the message of the Church which is meant to be prophetic lacks precisely the specific prophetic qualities.

The prophets are men who receive a word which is not their own. Their authority resides in their being sent by God. They speak because they are forced to speak. That is true of the Old Testament prophets; but just as much of St John writing down the Book of Revelation. And that is true of all prophets since. We have a classical example in John Knox. He tells himself the story of what he said to Mary, Queen of Scots: 'Your Grace accused me of having irreverently handled you in the pulpit; that I denied. Ye said, What ado had I to speak of your marriage? What was I, that I should mell with such matters? I answered that, as touching nature, I was a worm of this earth, and yet a subject of this commonwealth; but as touching the office wherein it had pleased God to place me, I was a watchman, both over the realm and over the Kirk of God gathered with the same. For that reason I was bound in conscience to blow the trumpet publicly, oft as ever I saw any upfall (i.e. incident), any appearing danger, either to the one or to the other.'[1]

The weakness in our speaking today lies in the absence of that burning sense of calling, of being overpowered by the

[1] *History of the Reformation of Religion in Scotland* by John Knox (edition of 1905), p. 298.

Word of God. And so the Church speaks all too often in a tone of well-meant advice rather than of eternal truth.

The prophetic office is the office of the watchman (Isa. 62.6; Jer. 6.17; Ezek. 3.17; 33.7). The watchman has two functions. He sees what is coming and he warns the people by blowing the trumpet. His attitude is one of expectancy. The prophet is turned towards the future. The prophetic office has an eschatological perspective. He is 'one who fore-tells the future activity of God in judgment upon the present by means of insight gained in the past'.[1] This finds expression in the Second Epistle of Peter where it is said of the prophetic word: 'You will do well to pay attention to this as to a lamp shining in a dark place, until the day dawns and the morning star rises in your hearts' (II Peter 1.19).

The prophetic message must therefore always be forward-looking. It must not recall men to a supposedly better past or seek to maintain an established order. It must be permeated by St Paul's 'one thing I do, forgetting what lies behind and straining forward to what lies ahead, I press on toward the goal for the prize of the upward call of God in Christ Jesus' (Phil. 3.13-14).

The weakness of much that the churches say to the world is precisely that it makes the impression of a harking back to a golden age rather than a hopeful turning to the future with the conviction that courageous deeds of justice and mercy will find their place in the great plan of salvation.

But it happens again and again that these same churches which seem to be so devoid of the prophetic sense are used to speak a clear Word of God to the world. We are privileged to live in a time when this actually takes place. I think of the witness which the Confessing Church of Germany and the churches of the occupied countries during the last war have

[1] John Marsh, *The Fullness of Time*, p. 56.

tendered with regard to the pagan ideology and the misdeeds of national socialism. I think especially of the church protests against the persecution of the Jews. I think of the action of the American churches (in the face of strong opposition) to ensure that their country should come to the rescue of the Indian people at the time of the great famine. I think of the voice of the Church in the Eastern Zone of Germany and its resistance against the totalitarian claims of dialectical materialism. And I would mention such resolutions of the Evanston Assembly of the World Council of Churches as those on race relations and on the international situation.

We must, however, not only think of such widely publicized examples. For the most important witness of the Christian Church is its local witness. When we speak of the Church as watchman or guardian in society, we must think very especially of its rôle in a given village or city, of its opportunity to speak out concerning the concrete spiritual and social needs in its immediate surroundings, of its privilege to demonstrate on the spot what true human solidarity means.

We have spoken of three ways in which the Lord of the Church uses our churches for his work in the world. We have reason to be gratefully astonished at his patience and mercy in that he continues to use these very imperfect instruments for his great purpose of salvation.

7

RENEWAL AND UNITY

THE history of the Church seems to teach us that there is a constant conflict between renewal and unity. There have been those in all ages for whom the whole emphasis in *Una Sancta* is on *Sancta* and there have been those to whom it is all important to maintain the Church's integrity as the *Una*. There have been those for whom the Church has no meaning unless it exemplifies the life of the new creation in constant renewal of life; there have been those to whom the Church as given in history is so precious that they look with suspicion upon any outbreak of new life which might affect the unity and peace of the Church. From the days of the Montanists, when Tertullian entered into conflict with the established hierarchy, till our own days, when groups break away from the historic churches to form sects exemplifying the new life of the spirit, the conflict has gone on in an almost monotonous fashion.

There are fanatics of renewal such as the Labadists in Holland in the seventeenth century who said that

> *Le mal est que le nom d'Église Réformée*
> *Fait croire qu'il suffit qu'on réforme en idée*

and proceeded to create a church in which the life of the whole as well as the life of each member was to manifest the total newness of the Church. And there are the fanatics of unity as the 'integralists' (not only in the Roman but also in other churches) who believe that the slightest deviation from accepted traditions is an attack on the Church itself and (to use words of Father Congar)[1] 'for whom everything which has come into existence after a certain date finds itself *ipso facto* in a state of mortal sin and damnation'.

The story of the conflict between unity and renewal has been described more than once, but the very way in which it has been written shows how difficult it is to take the two viewpoints seriously at the same time. Gottfrid Arnold, whose writings made such a deep impression on Goethe, called his history a *Non-partisan History of the Church and the Heresies* (1700) and pretended that his account of the heresies was really the first objective account of the great struggle between the Church and those who sought to change its doctrine or life. But the underlying presupposition of the whole work is that the institutional Church is always wrong, when it defends its unity and that true renewal of Christian life can only come through breaking away from all institutional religion. On the other hand R. A. Knox tells us in the preface of his book on *Enthusiasm* that at first he desired to write a trumpet blast against 'enthusiasm', but that as he pursued his studies, the men he had to write about became so human, that he became more concerned to find out why they thought as they did than to prove they were wrong. And his book is certainly unique in that a faithful member of a Church which according to his own statement is more institutional than all the other 'Christianities' shows penetrating insight into the thoughts and motivation of the so-called enthusiasts and even warns his fellow churchmen that the Church cannot live without enthusiasm. At the same time

[1] Conclusion of 'Vraie and Fausse Réforme dans l'Église' as translated in *Cross-currents*, 1951, 4.

the basic presupposition of the book is that Christianity is 'a balance of doctrines, and not merely of doctrines but of emphases' (p. 580), and that this balance is given in the teaching of the Roman Catholic Church. In other words the criterion of judgment is whether the unity created by this balance is maintained or disturbed. And the very title *Enthusiasm* which refers to a human attitude, obscures the fact that in many of the movements here described there is another factor at work, namely the gospel itself with its explicit insistence on the new life and the new creation.

Now it is a striking fact that in the Bible renewal and unity are not seen as alternatives or as competing objectives. On the contrary they are considered as interdependent, as two aspects of the work of God in and for his people. Thus the 'gathering' of the people, the reconstitution of their unity, to which the prophets look forward is far more than their being reassembled in the same place. It has always the overtone of the beginning of new life. The people will be gathered when they return unto the Lord (Deut. 30.2-3), when they keep his commandments (Neh. 1.9). The unity of the people under the coming messianic king, who will be their one shepherd, will be a unity in the observation of the statutes of the Lord (Ezek. 37.24).

The well-known vision of Ezekiel concerning the dry bones provides a further illustration. He sees the bones coming together. They are again covered by sinews and flesh and skin. But that is not sufficient, for there is no breath in them (Ezek. 37.8). Unity by itself is nothing, may even mean death. It is only when the breath of God comes upon the bones that 'the whole house of Israel' is truly gathered and united. Unity in the biblical sense is God-given unity which implies new life.

In the New Testament the togetherness of the two comes out even more clearly. In Romans 12 the call to the faithful to let their lives be transformed by the renewal of their mind is made specific and concrete in the description of the true unity through the interchange and interplay of the spiritual gifts. In Ephesians 2.15 the oneness of Jew and Gentile in the Church is described as the creation of one new man in place of two. And in this expression we have the strongest possible affirmation that renewal is to participate in the life of the new community, which finds its unity in Christ, and that the unity of that community is unity in the newness of life which Christ incarnates and communicates to those who believe in him.

The Gospel of John provides further evidence. In the high-priestly prayer our Lord prays (John 17.22-23) according to the translation of William Temple: 'And the glory which thou hast given to me I have given to them that they may be one as we are one—I in them and thou in me, that they may be perfected into one. . . .' The true unity is the consequence of the *doxa*, the glory, which is the quality of life of the new creation in Christ. The Lord prays that the plan of God may be brought to its final consummation and that consummation is the total newness of the faithful in perfect unity, a unity which consists in sharing in the glory of the new creation. Now it has often been suggested that this profound unity can only be understood as a spiritual and invisible unity. But that is to deny the very evidence of the text. For this perfect unity is, according to the words of the prayer, to convince the world that God has sent Christ and thus revealed his love for the world. As Temple observes: 'there is offered something for the world to see, namely the glory which the Father gave to the Son and the Son to the disciples'. The unity of which the New Testament speaks is at the same time the most deeply spiritual unity and the most tangible, incarnate unity.

Both unity and renewal are divine gifts. The Epistle to Titus (3.5), speaks of 'renewal of the Holy Spirit' and the Epistle to the Ephesians (4.3) of the 'unity of the Holy Spirit'. These parallel expressions mean that renewal and unity are both created by the Holy Spirit, the giver of life and the builder of the Church.

Why is it then that two intrinsic qualities of the Church which are so closely related to each other in the New Testament, appear to us as alternatives or even as mutually exclusive goals? I believe that the reason is that we have consciously or unconsciously secularized both notions. I take secularizing in its literal meaning of adaptation to this age as opposed to orientation toward the new age. It is our lack of a truly eschatological perspective which makes it so hard to take renewal as seriously as unity and unity as seriously as renewal.

We have already seen that renewal in the biblical sense is something quite different from renewal on the purely historical level. True renewal is not to be equated with adaptation to a changed situation, with a passing from lethargy to activism, with a change of structure or with new forms of expression. Far too often these signs of life, or (to use the phrase of R. A. Knox) these forms of enthusiasm, which may very well be mere signs of the vitality of natural man, have been taken or are taken as evidence, that a true reformation or renewal of the Church takes place. The criterion of renewal, it cannot be said too strongly, is the newness of the new creation. The real issue is whether the Church lives up to its calling to be the representative on earth of the new age which has begun in Christ.

In the same way we have to de-secularize our thinking

about unity. We must not think of it in merely institutional terms. For institutional unity may be very worldly unity. Like newness, unity is rooted in the new age, in the unity which characterizes the life of the Kingdom. This unity enters into our age through the Church and it is therefore by no means a 'Platonic' ideal or a merely invisible thing. But its source and criterion are not historical or sociological. We are truly one only when our unity reflects that unity which the Son has with the Father and which he gives to those who belong to him.

It is then only if we seek again to recapture the eschatological dimensions of the New Testament that we may hope to find a way out of the dilemma which the conflict of unity and renewal has created for us.

These are not merely theological considerations. They have a very practical bearing on the life of our churches as they participate together in the ecumenical movement. If we have rightly interpreted the biblical teaching, the ecumenical movement must be concerned with renewal as well as with unity. We think and talk too much about the ecumenical movement, as if it were only interested in the unity of the Church. As a matter of fact it has never concentrated exclusively on the reunion of the churches. The unofficial slogan of the Oxford Conference of 1937, 'let the Church be the Church' was in fact an expression of a deep and widespread awareness that the churches stood in need of a radical renewal. This conviction was all the stronger because it grew out of a return to biblical theology. Men and women of differing confessions who could not see their way to agreement on the form and order of the Church, were united in their new understanding of the Church as 'a peculiar people' or (as Moffatt has it) 'the people who belong to him' (I Peter 2.9) and which is therefore not to be conformed to this world, but to be constantly transformed by the renewal of its mind. Again the struggle of the Confessing churches in Germany, and in several occupied countries, helped many to understand that the unity which the churches must seek is not unity at any price, but on the contrary unity in deeper common understanding of the specific nature and mission of the Church. And this has found expression in the life of the World Council of Churches. The 'Call to the Churches' concerning its first assembly said: 'We have failed because we ourselves have been partakers in man's disorder. Our first and deepest need is not new organization, but the renewal, or rather the rebirth, of the actual churches. May God grant that we hear the call of the Spirit.' That is also why in the programme of the World Council there is a strong emphasis on those aspects of the life of the Church such as evangelism, the mission of the laity, the relations of men and women, in which the renewal of the Church must become manifest. And when 'Faith and Order', seeking to advance the cause of unity, deals with the 'social and cultural factors' which prove to be tenacious obstacles to unity, it is in fact challenging the churches to disentangle themselves from their alliances with the old world and to become churches of the new age.

In the same way recent ecumenical history has made us understand better that the gift of renewal like every spiritual gift is given 'for the common good' (I Cor. 12.7), that is for the upbuilding of the whole body in its unity. It has always been true that renewal in one church tended to call forth renewal in other churches and that in this way a new sense of belonging together across confessional frontiers was created. But that process of sharing has been intensified and widened as the churches have been drawn out of their isolation into ecumenical relationships. The churches have now an opportunity of letting themselves be challenged by those signs of renewal which take place in other parts of the total fellowship. And as the sense of responsibility for each other and solidarity with each other grows, we learn at the same time that renewal is not necessarily renewal *against* those who are considered to be living in conformity to the world, but renewal for the sake of the whole.

But if it is now widely understood that unity and renewal belong together, that does not yet mean that it is clearly understood how they are related to each other and how, as we tried to show, both are essential aspects of that eschatological life which the Church is called to live. At this point we can only say that there are signs that the rediscovery of that neglected dimension of the Church's life is taking place. The Report on the main theme of the Evanston Assembly was, in spite of all criticisms directed against it, a document of very considerable ecumenical importance in that it showed so clearly what this rediscovery may mean for the whole life and message of the churches. The urgent question is whether the churches will come to realize that they can have neither renewal nor unity unless they accept to live the hopeful and expectant life, praying constantly for the gift of newness and unity, and unless in order to render their truest service to the world they are ready to be less at home in the world. 'Let the Church be the Church' means: let the Church be the pilgrim people of God tasting and demonstrating the powers of the age to come; let it truly believe that, in the words of the report to the Evanston Assembly, 'God acts from moment to moment and from generation to generation, re-creating the Church ever anew by the Spirit who indwells it, renewing its faithfulness, its purity, its self-sacrifice, its courage.'

INDEX OF NAMES

INDEX OF BIBLICAL REFERENCES